CALIFORNIA PRISON POLAROIDS

Eric "Superman" Sturgess

Rose Of Sharon
PUBLISHING

ERIC "SUPERMAN" STURGESS

Printed Worldwide
First Printing 2025
First Edition 2025

10 9 8 7 6 5 4 3 2 1

Rose of Sharon Publishing books may be ordered through booksellers or by contacting:

Rose Of Sharon Publishing
roseofsharonpublishing.com
P.O. Box 186
Floresville, Texas 78114

ISBN: 978-1-970335-09-5 Paperback

Preface

Growing up in the 1970s and 1980s, Polaroid pictures were a common sight. I was always fascinated by them and how the picture slowly appeared over time. People would swing the photo back and forth like a hand fan to supposedly make the image appear quicker.

I have been collecting Polaroid pictures of convicts in the California Department of Corrections and Rehabilitation for several years now. They are rare and hard to find after all these years. The 1990s were the last decade when Polaroid pictures were commonly used in California state prisons.

These photos are a snapshot of time that captures these men doing their best to survive behind those cold prison walls. These photos and the people in them deserve to be seen by others and their lives not forgotten in the dustbins of history. It just reminds us how fleeting our lives are. Nobody is guaranteed tomorrow, and our youth quickly fades to old age if we are blessed to live that long.

God bless you
Eric Sturgess
Romans 10:9-13

Table of Contents

Introduction

The Polaroid camera was never meant to be an archive of prison life. It was marketed as instant fun — snapshots of birthdays, vacations, and family gatherings. But inside California's prisons, the same instant film became something different. For many incarcerated men, a Polaroid was the only way to send a face home, the only tangible evidence that they were still alive behind the walls.

These images were not taken by professional photographers or staged for history books. They were created in visiting rooms, in yards, or against cinderblock walls with nothing but fluorescent light overhead. A few might show smiles, carefully pressed shirts, or arm-in-arm poses with loved ones. Others reveal the tension of survival — tattoos, hardened stares, and the weight of years still to be served. Each photo carries the marks of its environment: the faded color, the worn corners, the roughness of time.

California's prison system in the late twentieth century was notorious. Places like San Quentin, Folsom, Tracy, and Soledad earned reputations for violence and overcrowding, becoming known as gladiator schools where survival meant toughness. For those living inside, a camera was rare, and a Polaroid became both a lifeline and a shield. To mail a photo home was to remind family that you still existed. To keep one tucked in a book or on a cell wall was to hold on to identity in a place designed to strip it away.

These Polaroids show us more than uniforms and tattoos; they reveal the human face of incarceration. A man might project pride, defiance, or humor in front of the lens, but behind that single frozen frame is a story we cannot fully see — the circumstances that led him inside, the years endured, the family waiting outside, the dreams long abandoned or still clung to in secret.

This collection does not claim to tell the whole truth of prison life. No single image can. What it does is capture moments otherwise lost — faces and fragments that remind us that history is not only written in official records, but also in the small, fragile keepsakes that survive against the odds.

These Polaroids are artifacts of a hidden world, documents of resilience and confinement, and evidence of how human beings find ways to be remembered, even in the harshest places.

To look at them is to confront both the distance and the closeness of prison life. The distance lies in the razor wire, the walls, and the label of "inmate." The closeness lies in the eyes, in the hands folded or fists clenched, in the attempt to hold dignity in a place designed to break it. The instant camera may have been simple, but in these pictures, it became something profound: a tool of memory, survival, and truth.

The use of Polaroid cameras in California prisons peaked between the 1970s and 1990s, when film was cheap, instant photography was widely available, and prison regulations were looser about what could pass in and out of visiting rooms. By the early 2000s, digital security measures, policy shifts, and the decline of Polaroid itself ended the practice. What remains today are these fragile photographs — snapshots that outlasted their era, offering us a rare and unfiltered glimpse into prison life during one of California's most turbulent decades of incarceration.

Photographs

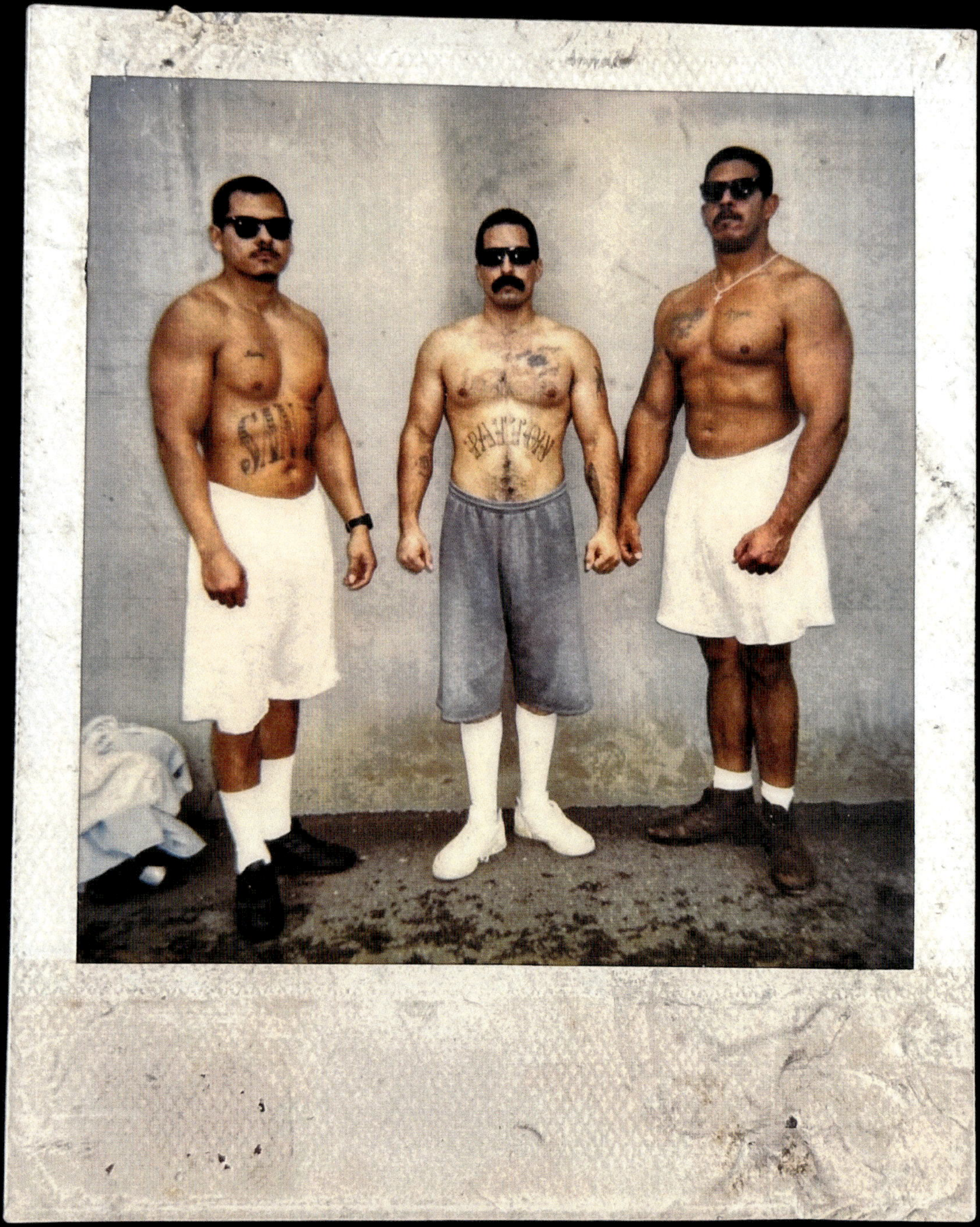

This picture is from the early 1990s and there are three Northerners pictured. The weights were taken away around 1996 in the California Department of Corrections. These dudes obviously spent lots of time on the weight pile.

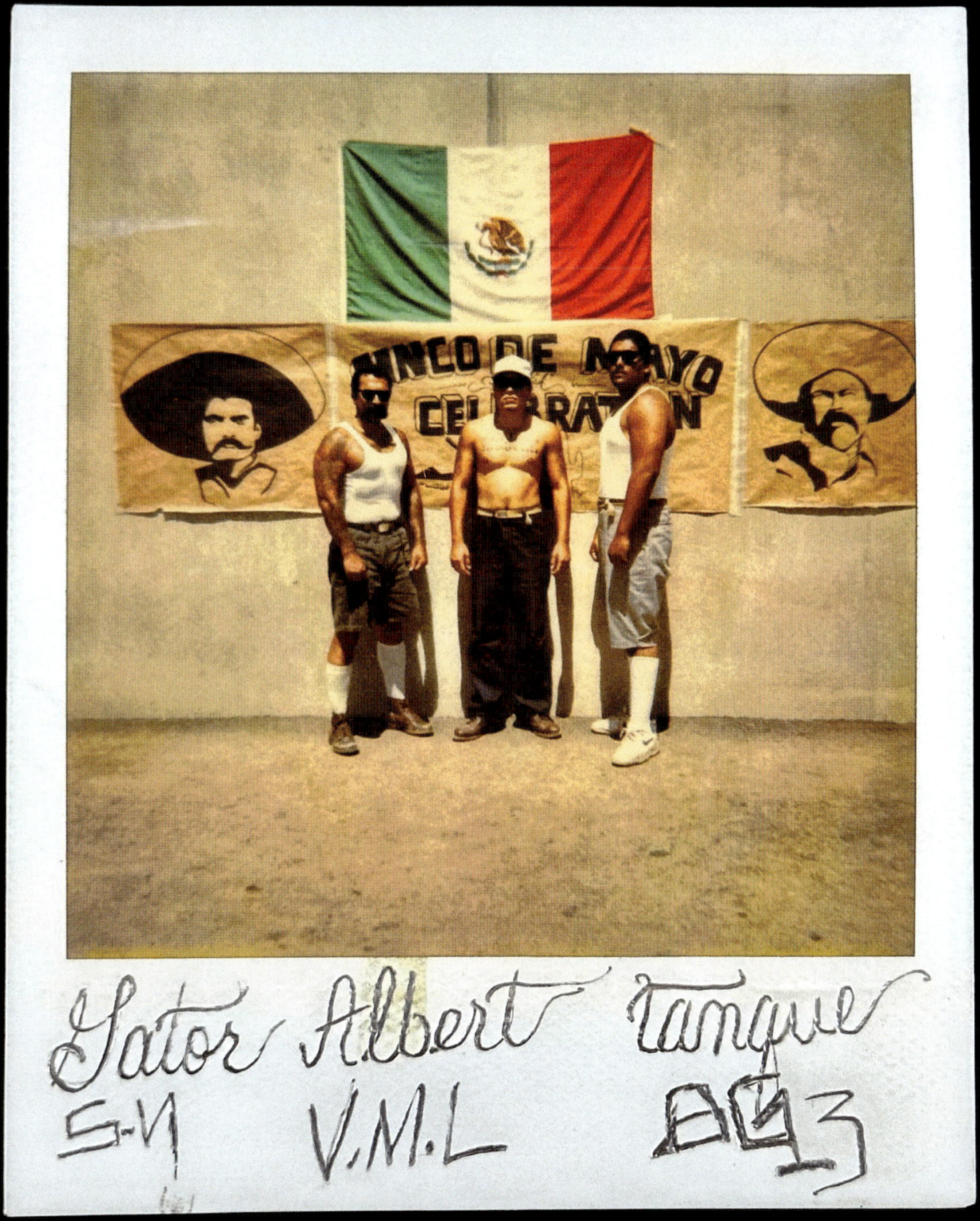

This is a Cinco De Mayo celebration depicting three Southerners at an unknown California prison in the early 1990s. A Southerner is a Hispanic Gang member from Southern California who, in prison, is under the authority of the Mexican Mafia.

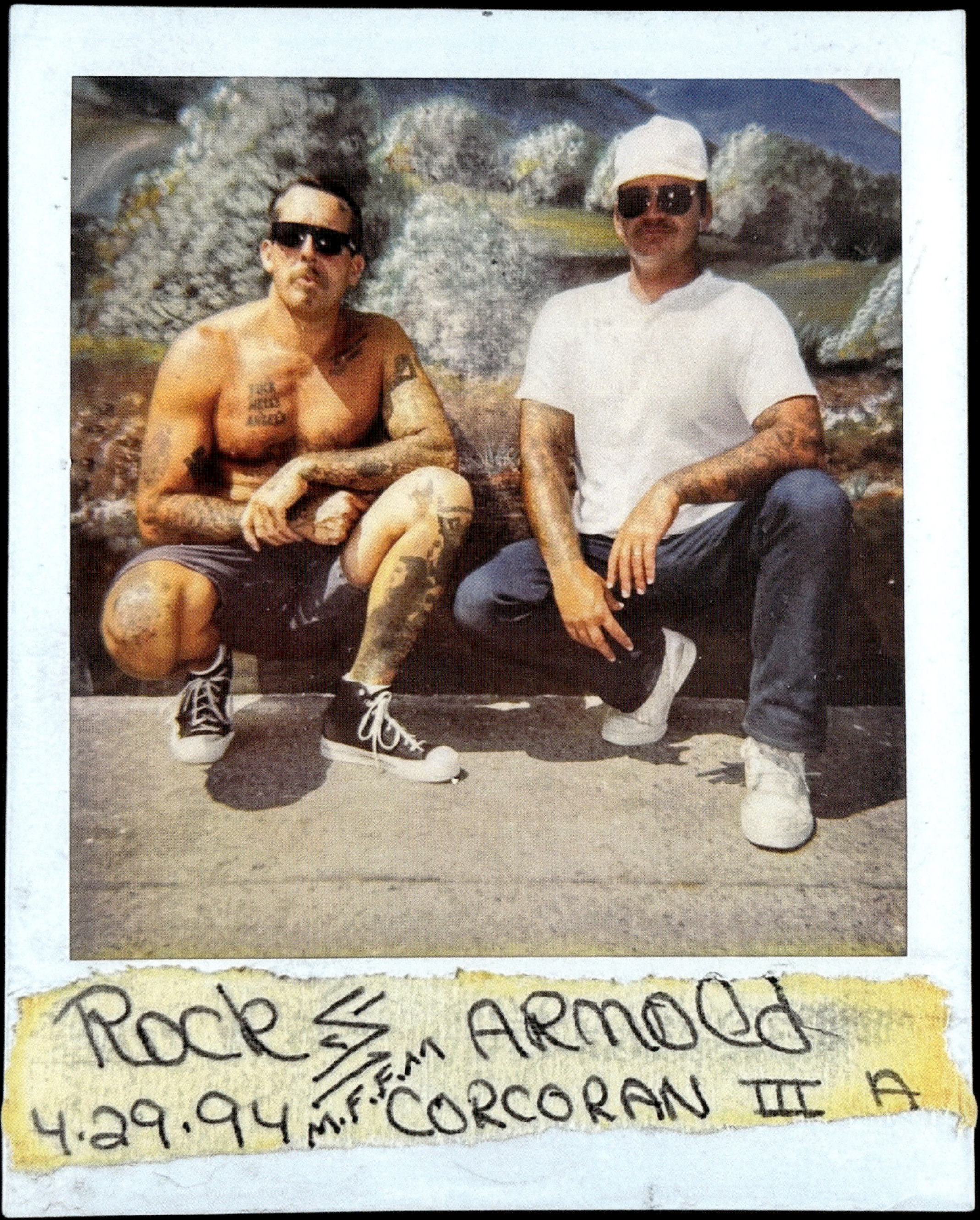

This photo depicts two Peckerwoods at Corcoran State Prison in 1994. The dude on the left is a Mongol and he has a tattoo on his right chest that says, "F**k Hells Angels." He also has a swastika on his right bicep.

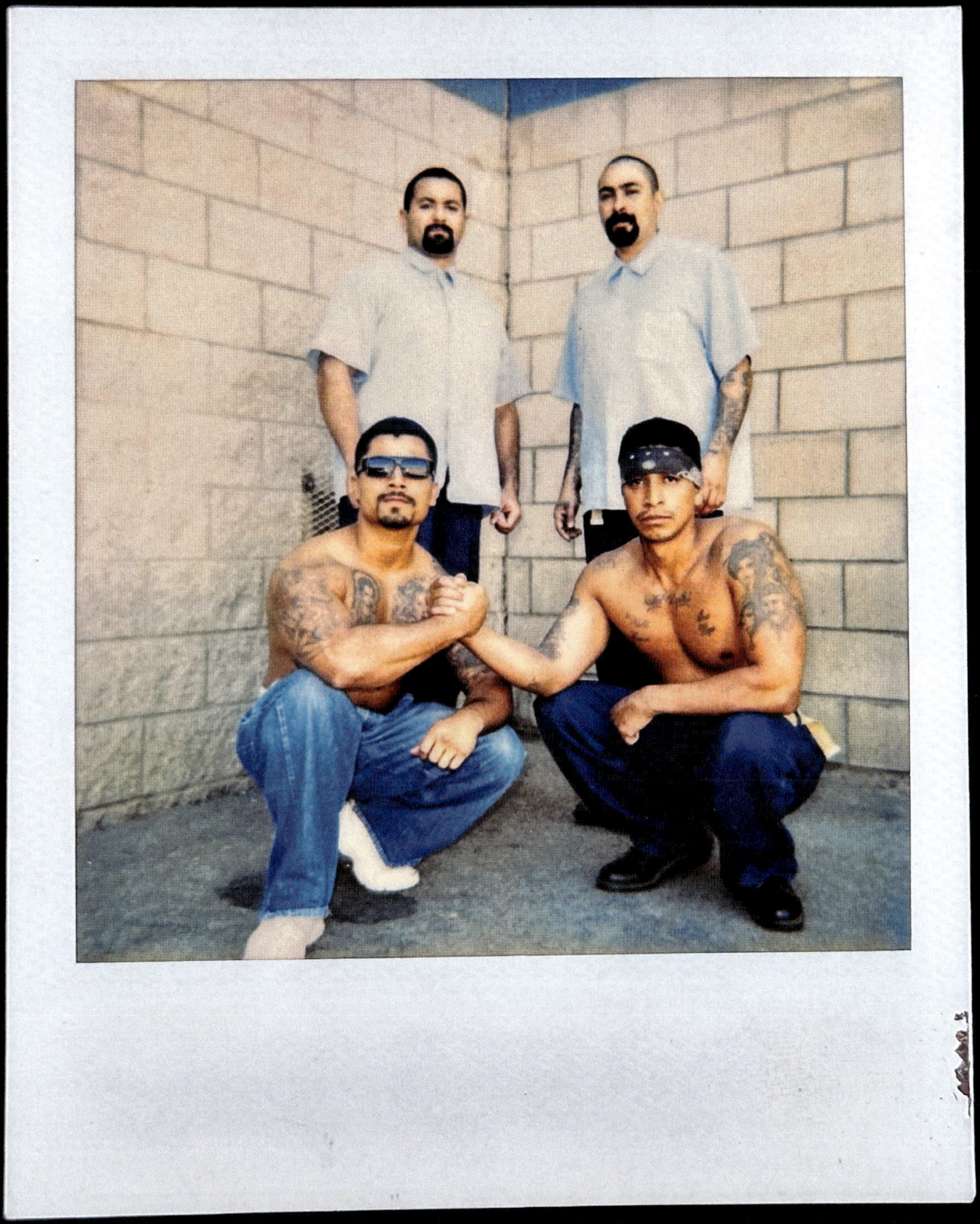

This photo, taken in the late 1990s, depicts four Southerners in classic prison poses. A Southerner is a Hispanic Gang member from Southern California who, in prison, is under the authority of the Mexican Mafia.

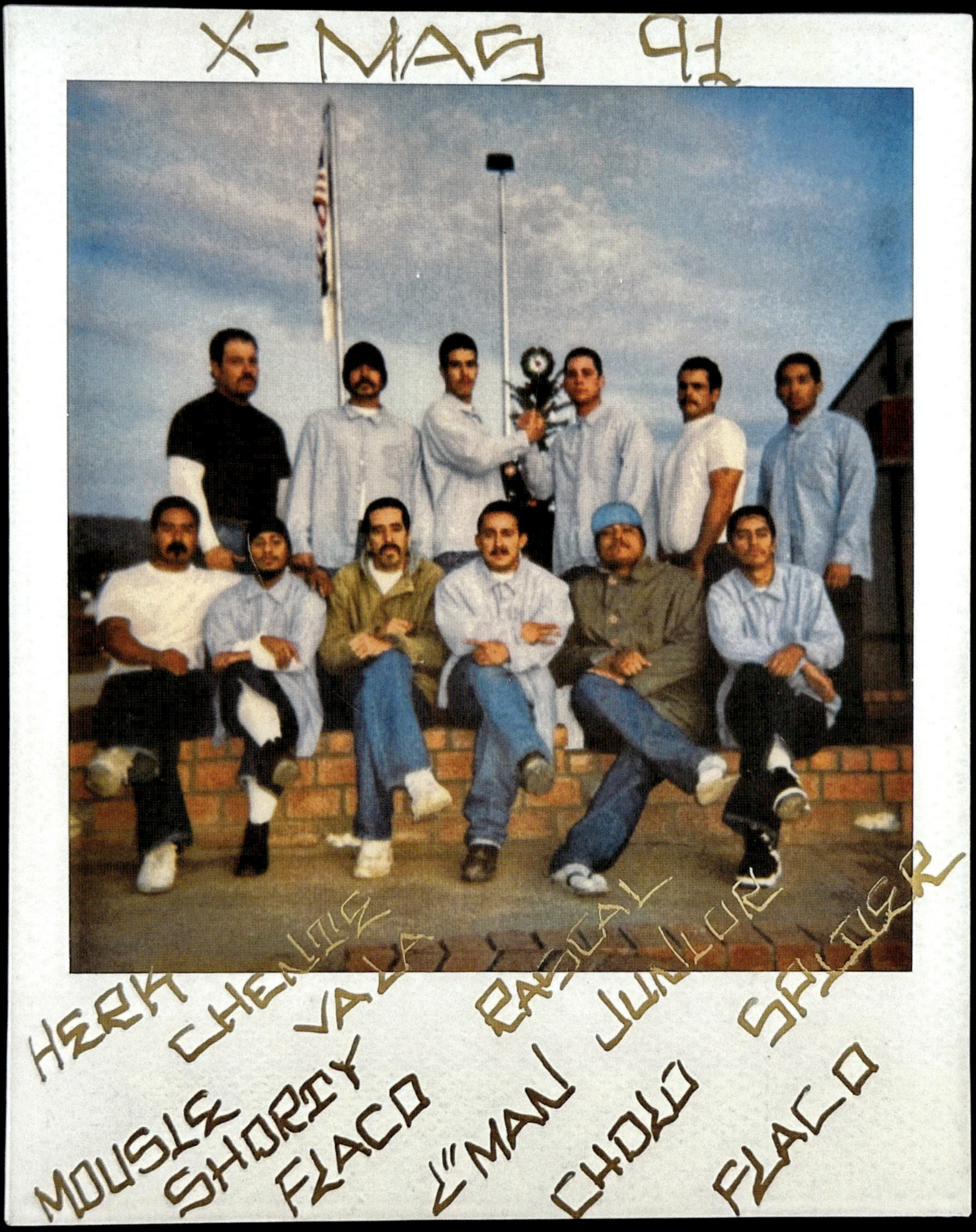

This photo is from Christmas in 1991 from an unknown California prison and a group of Southerners are pictured. A Southerner is a Hispanic Gang member from Southern California who, in prison, is under the authority of the Mexican Mafia.

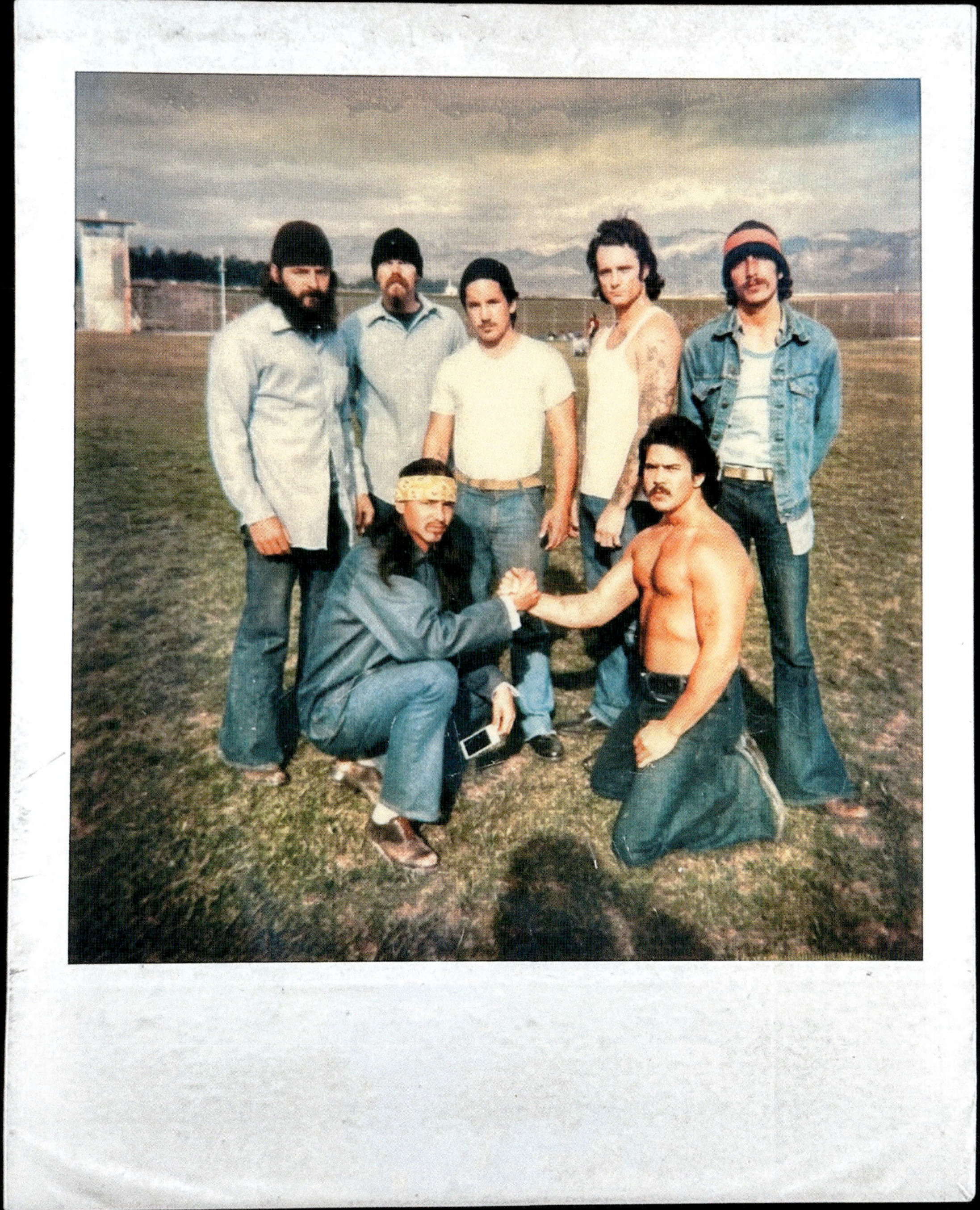

This photo is from the late 1970s at Deuel Vocational Institute (DVI also called Tracy). Pictured are a group of Peckerwoods (Woods). Woods are what affiliated White convicts are called in the California Department of Corrections and Rehabilitation.

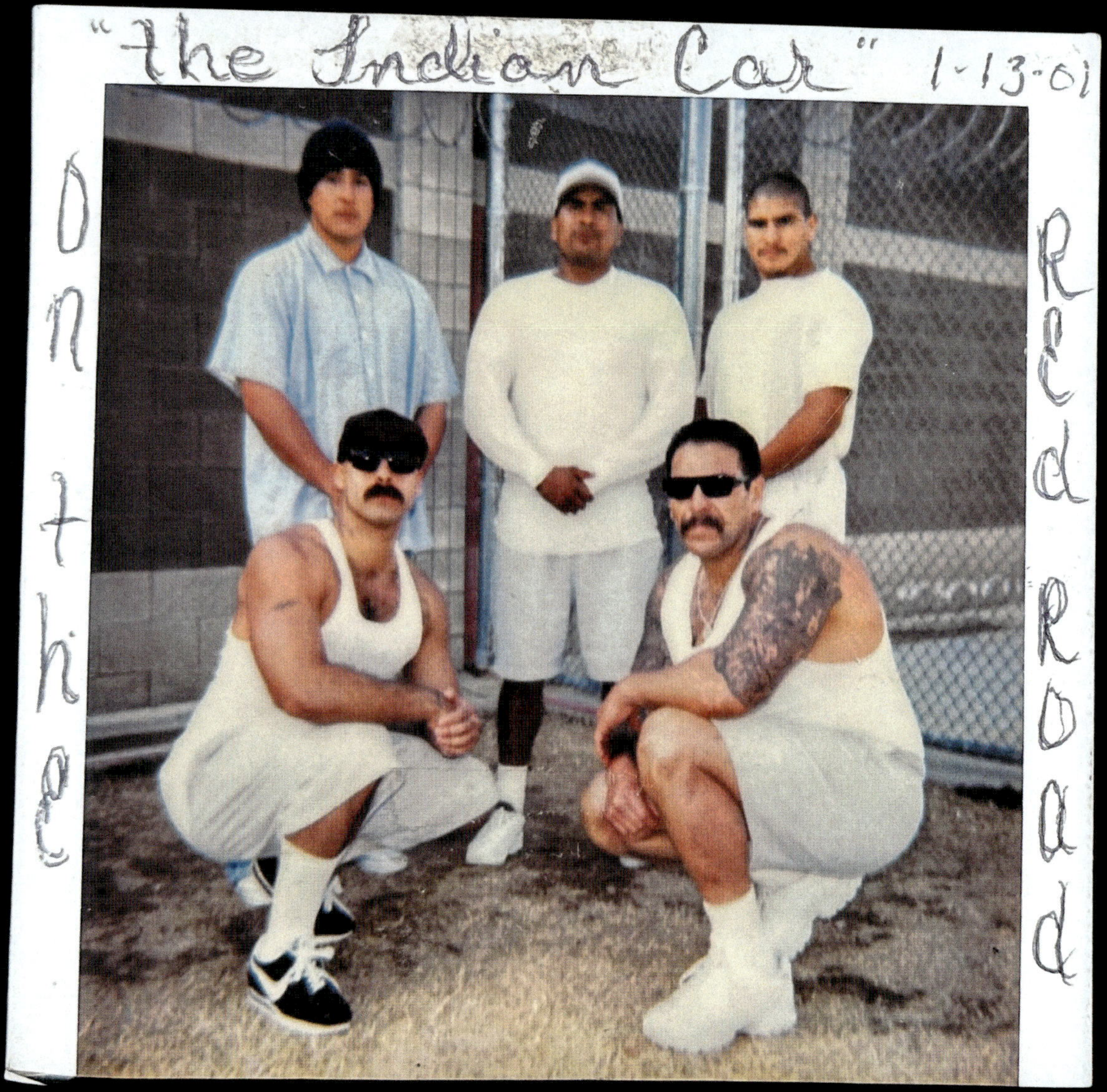

This photo is from 2001 from an undisclosed California prison. The Red Road refers to Native Americans and a group of them are pictured. In the California Department of Corrections and Rehabilitation Native Americans have their own area where they can do their ceremonies in a sweat lodge.

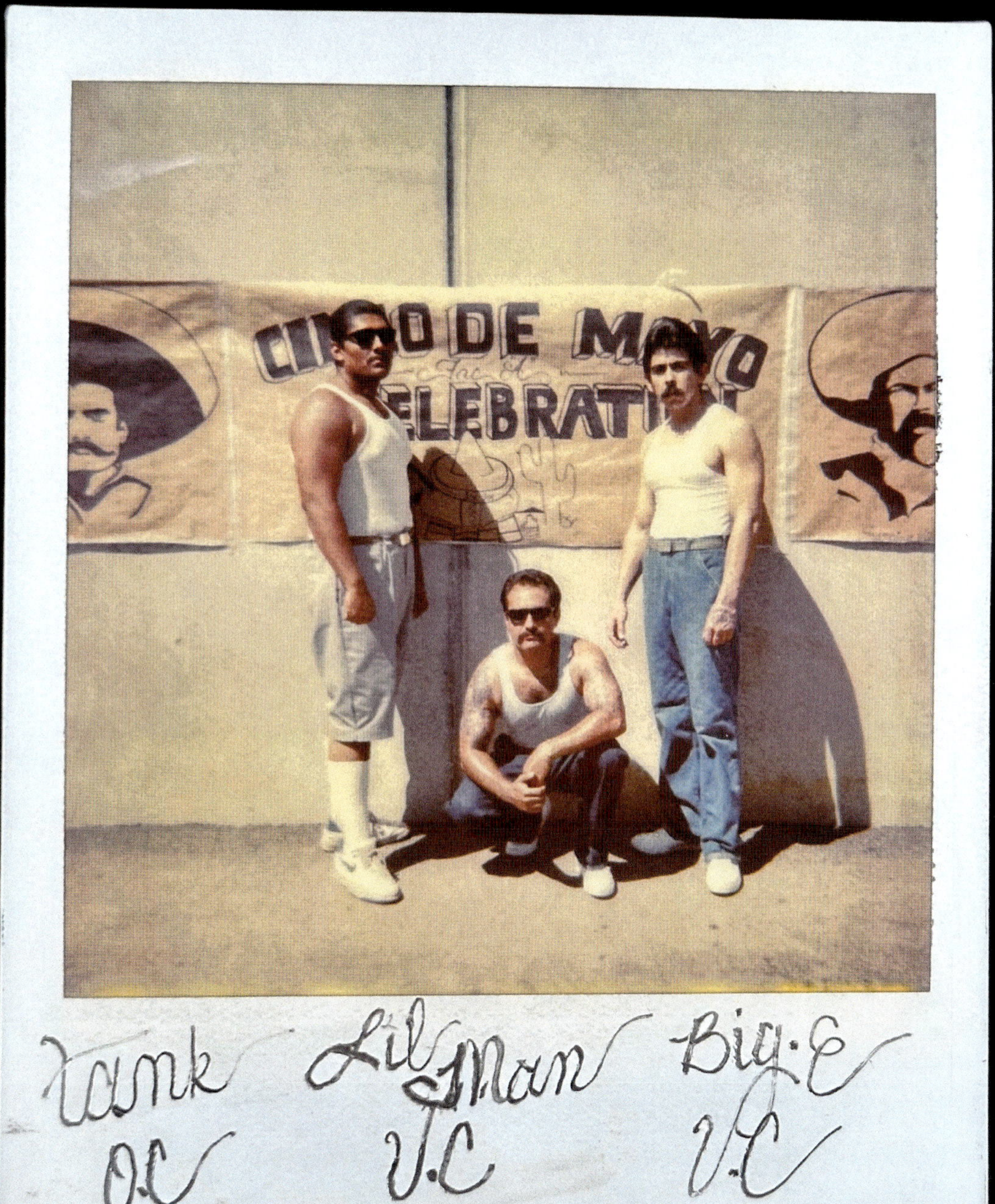

This is a Cinco De Mayo celebration depicting three Southerners at an unknown California prison in the early 1990s. A Southerner is a Hispanic Gang member from Southern California who, in prison, is under the authority of the Mexican Mafia.

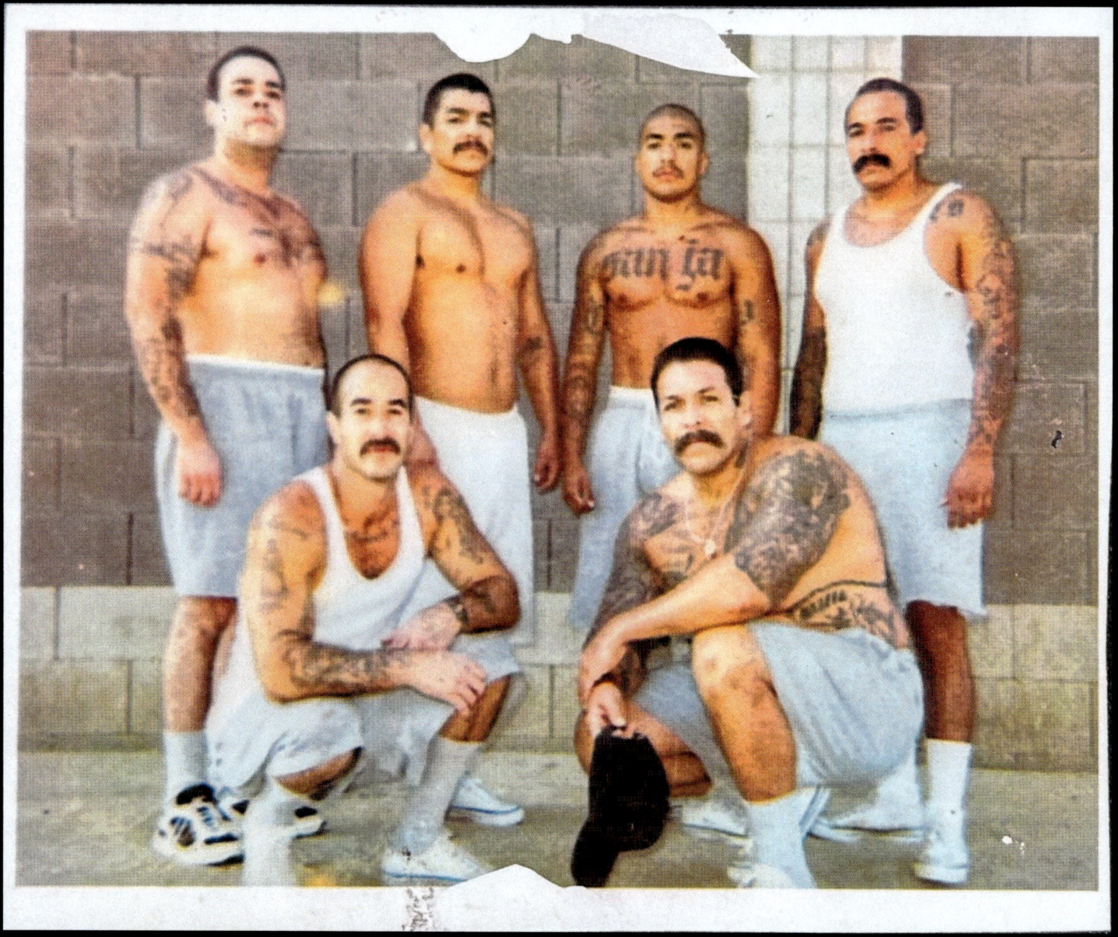

This photo was taken in 1991 on an unknown California prison yard.

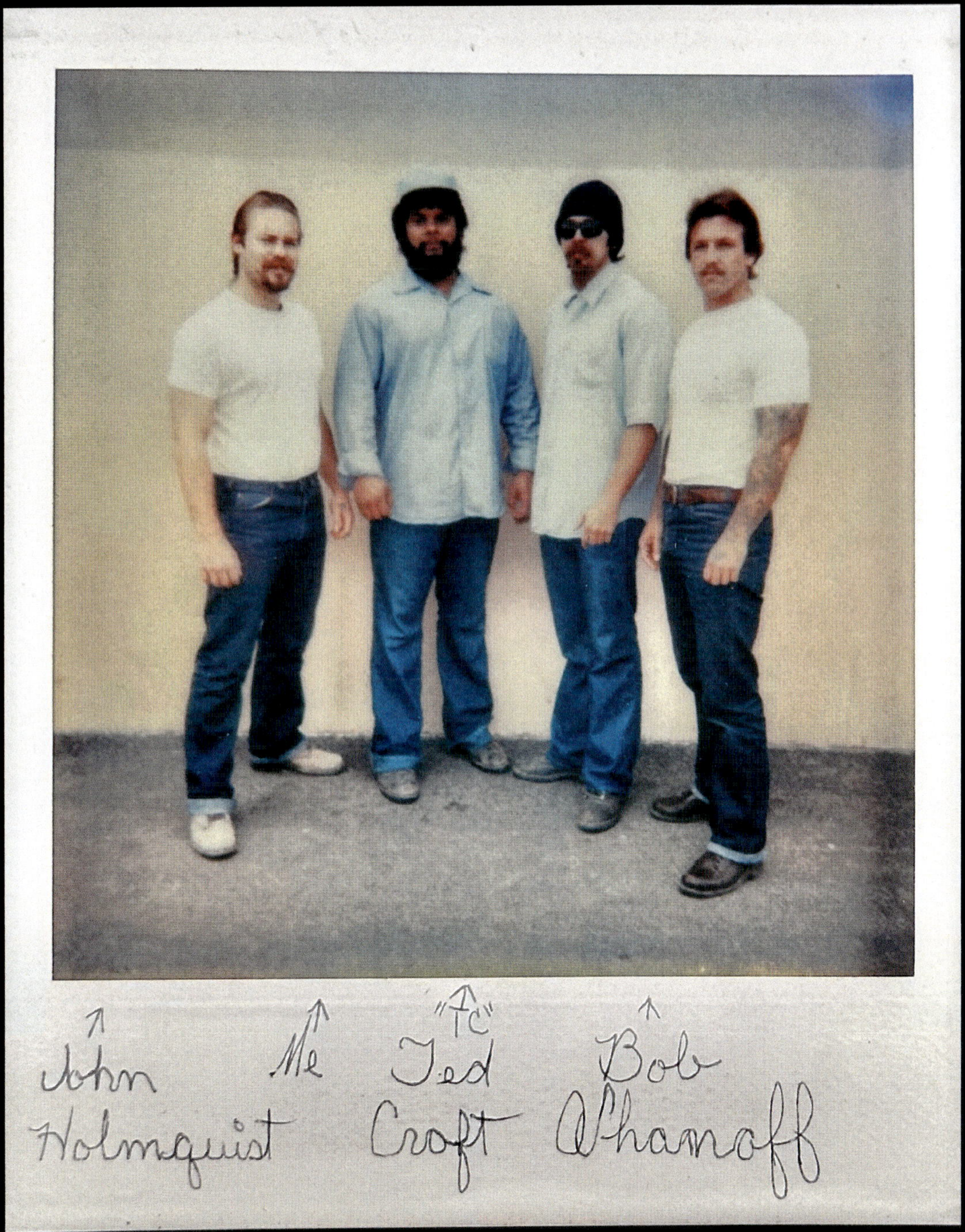

This photo was taken at Sierra Conservation Center State Prison (Jamestown) in the late 1990s. Pictured are a group of Peckerwoods (Woods). Woods are affiliated White convicts who are under the authority of the Aryan Brotherhood.

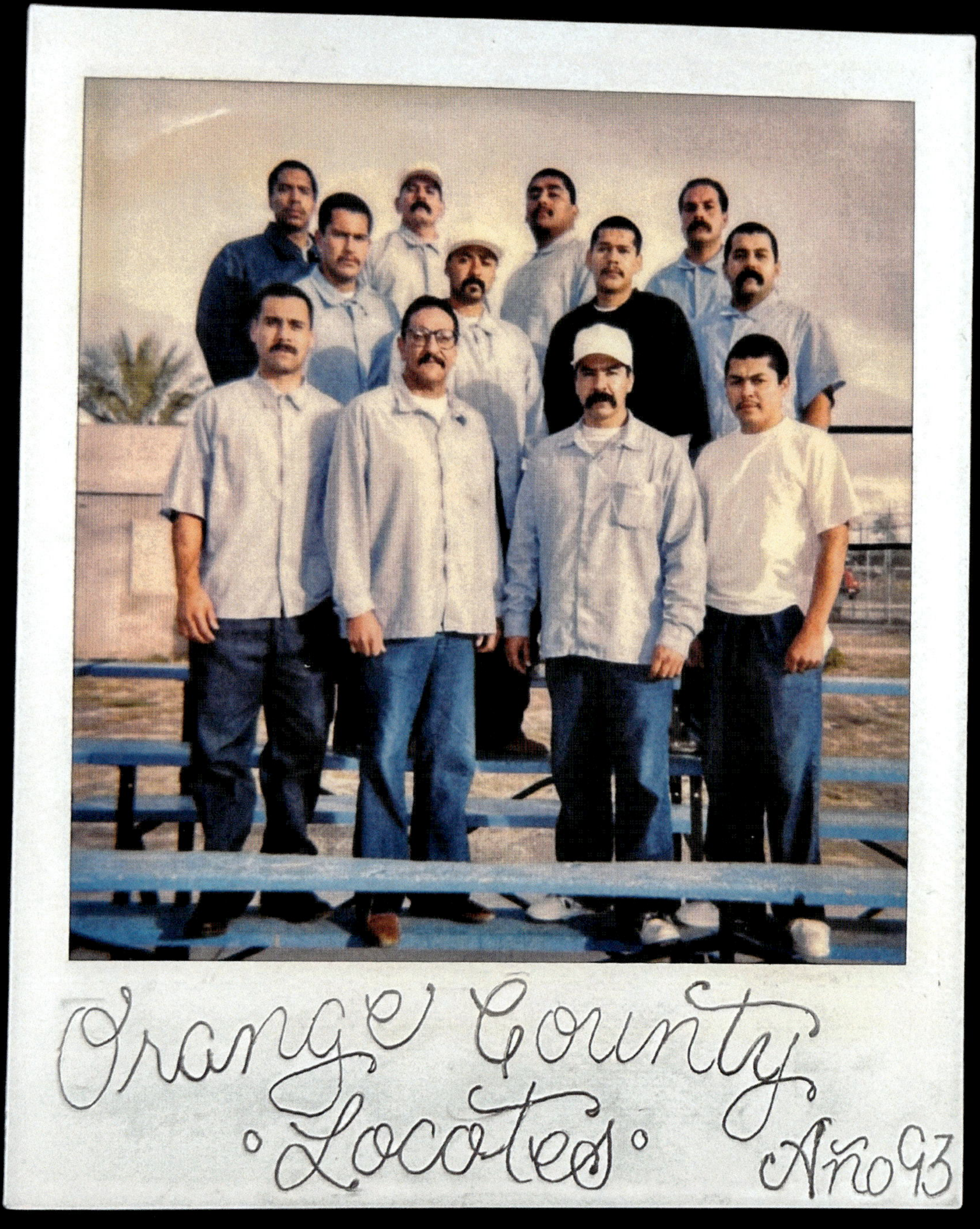

This photo, taken in the late 1990s, depicts a group of Southerners in classic prison poses. A Southerner is a Hispanic Gang member from Southern California who, in prison, is under the authority of the Mexican Mafia.

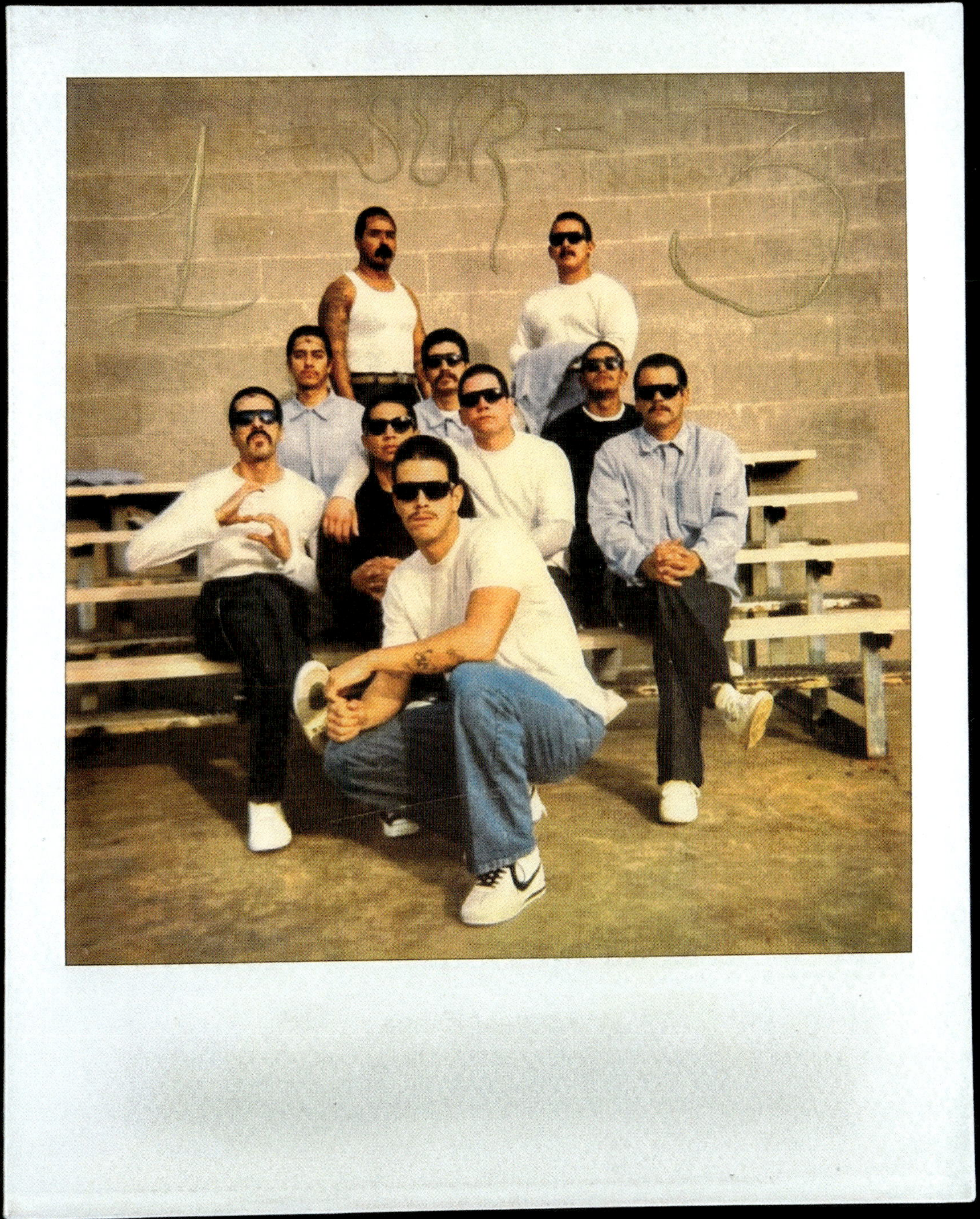

This photo, taken in the mid-1990s, depicts a group of Southerners in classic prison poses. A Southerner is a Hispanic Gang member from Southern California who, in prison, is under the authority of the Mexican Mafia.

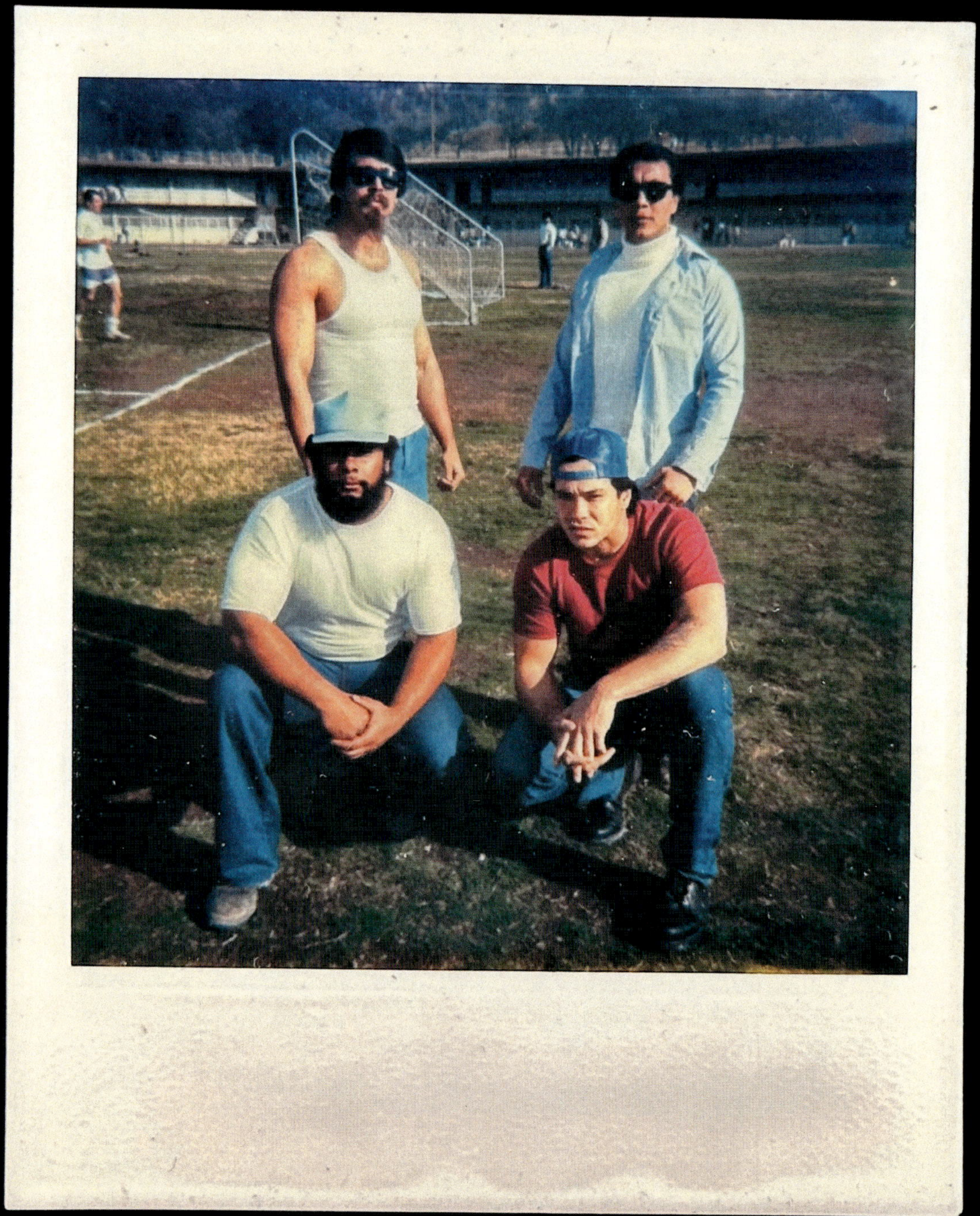

This photo was taken at Sierra Conservation Center State Prison (Jamestown) in the late 1990s. Pictured are a group of convicts on the prison yard.

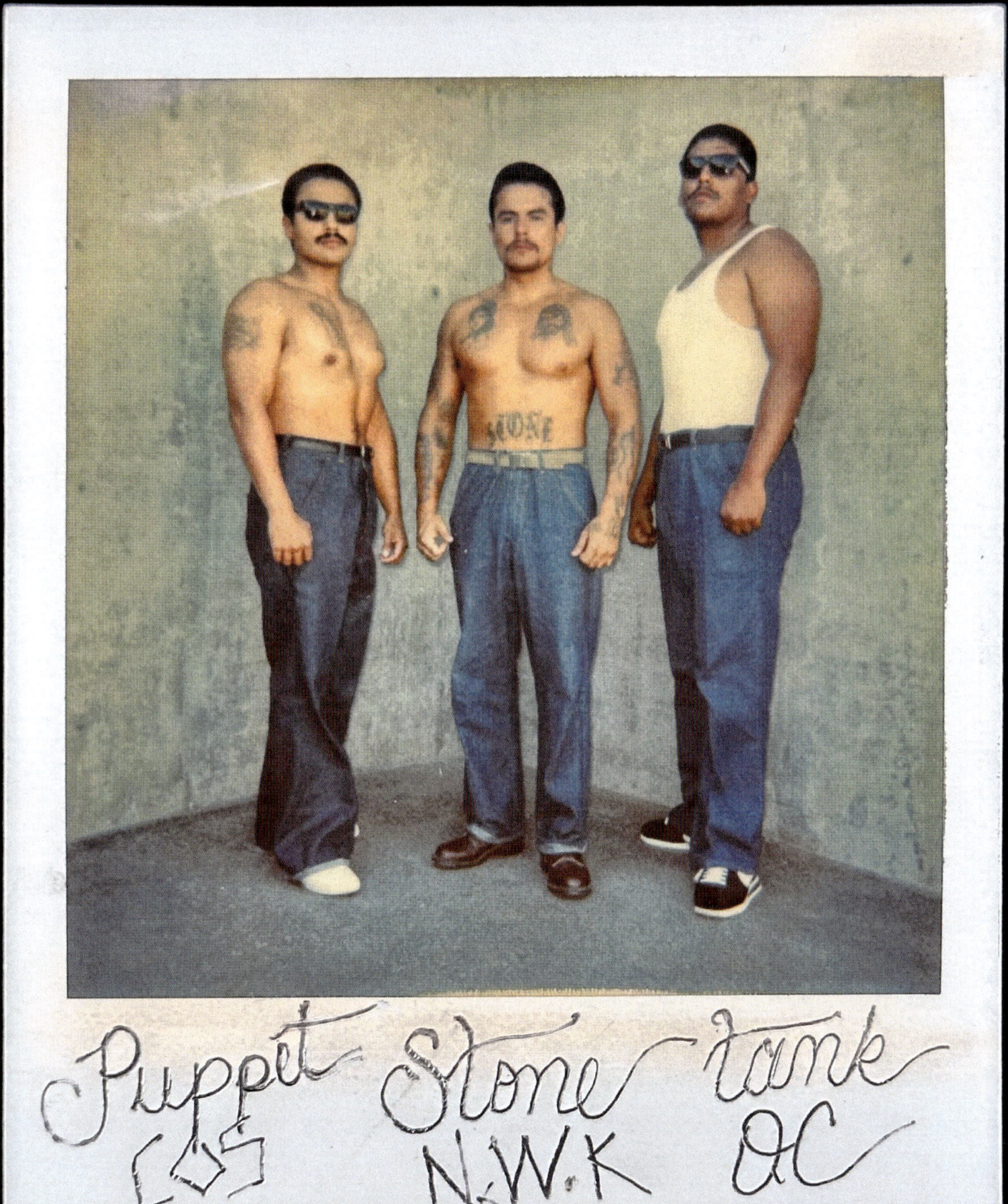

This photo, taken in the mid-1990s, depicts a group of Southerners in classic prison poses. A Southerner is a Hispanic Gang member from Southern California who, in prison, is under the authority of the Mexican Mafia.

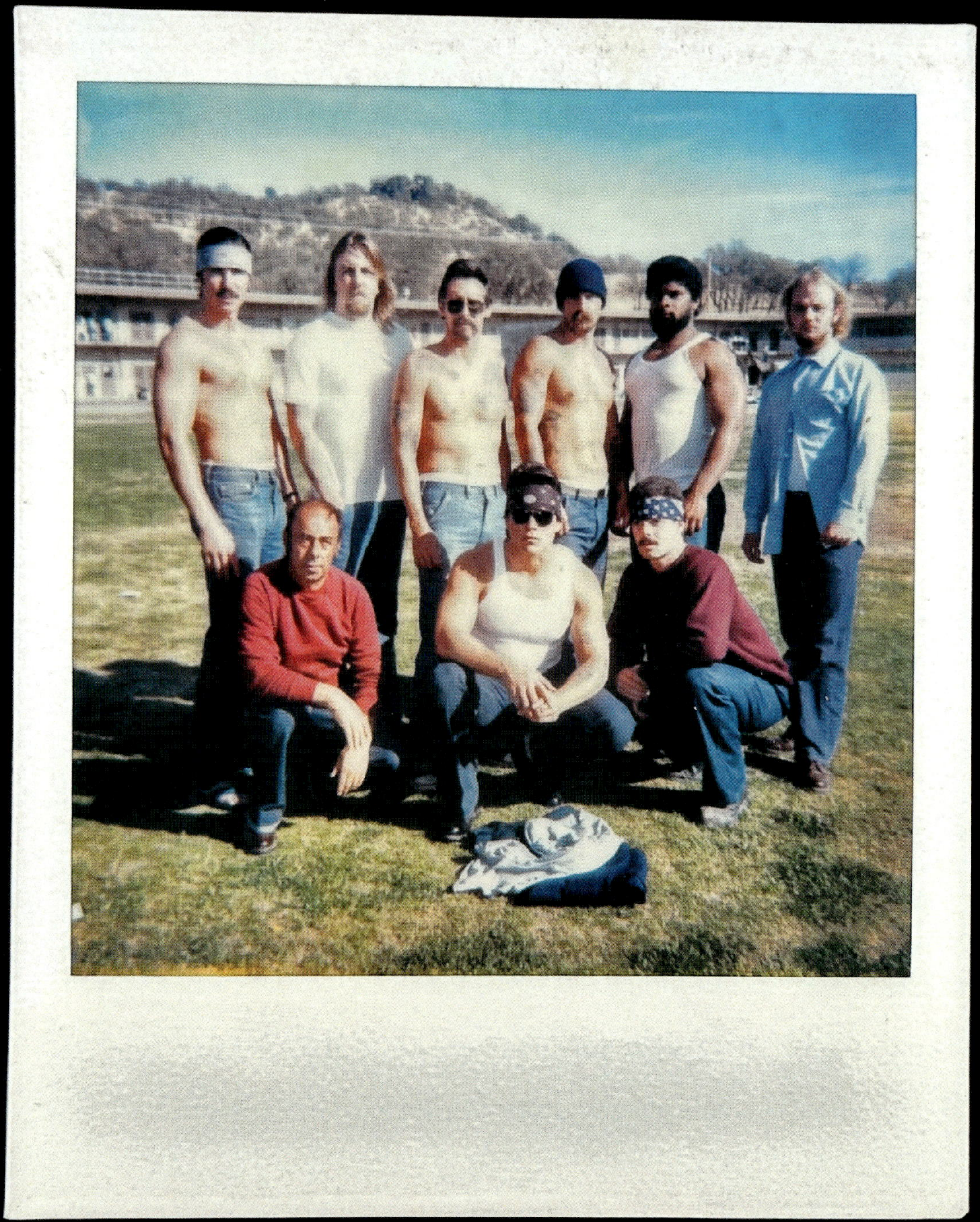

This photo was taken at Sierra Conservation Center State Prison (Jamestown) in the late 1990s. Pictured are a group of Peckerwoods (Woods). Woods are affiliated White convicts who are under the authority of the Aryan Brotherhood.

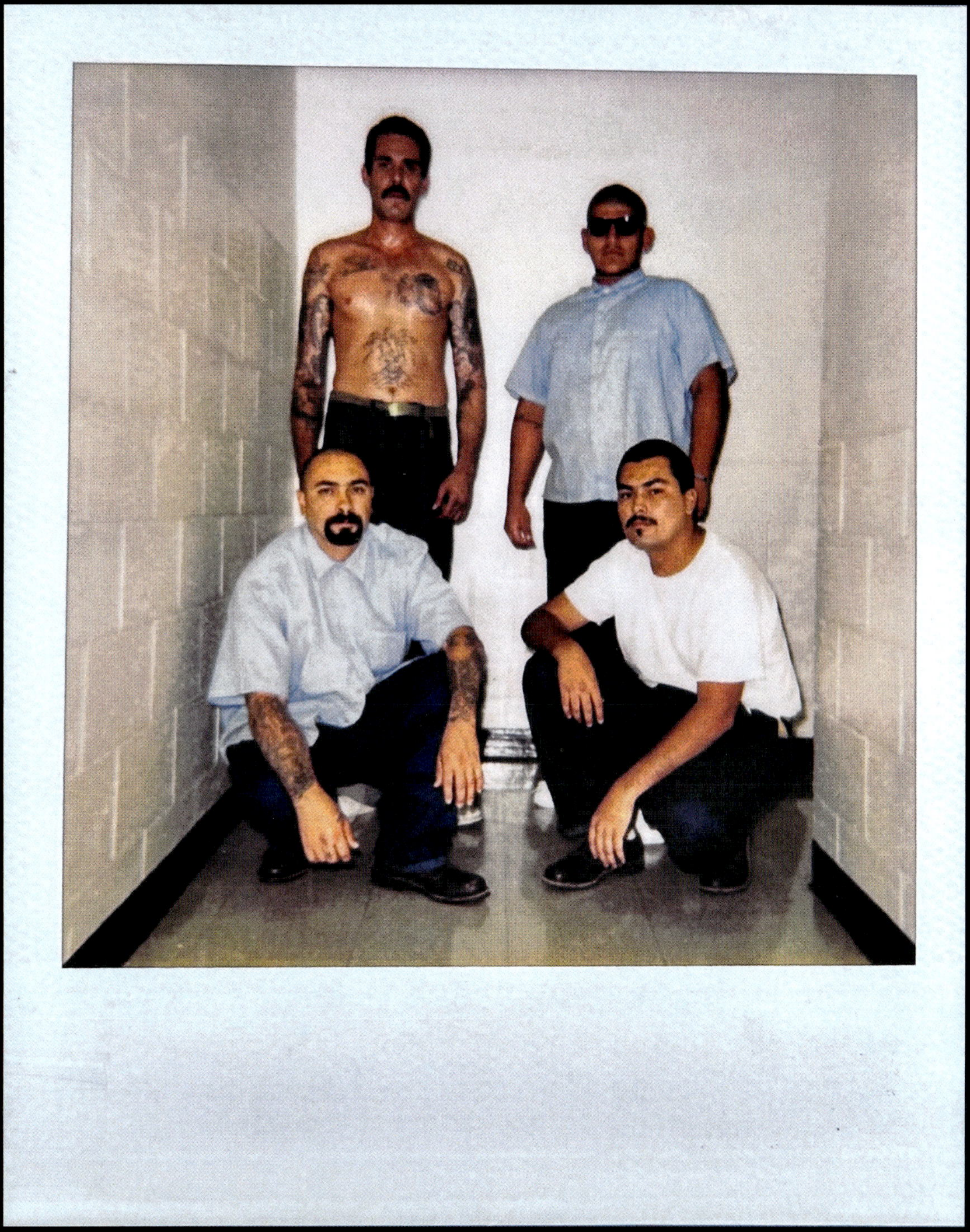

This photo, taken in the mid-1990s, depicts a group of Southerners in classic prison poses. A Southerner is a Hispanic Gang member from Southern California who, in prison, is under the authority of the Mexican Mafia.

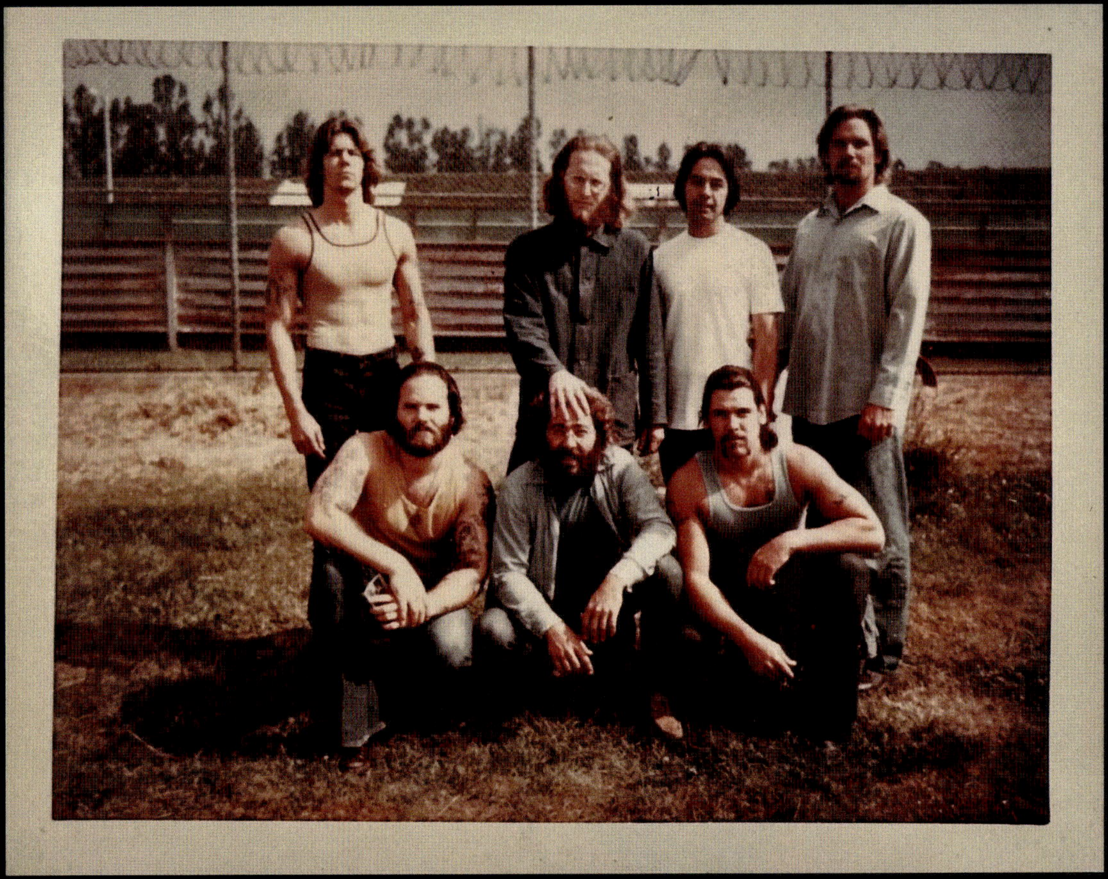

This photo was taken at Soledad State Prison on May 9, 1976. Pictured are a group of Peckerwoods (Woods) from Orange County. Some of the names on the back of the photo are: Joker, Flash, Bo Bo, Danny, Don, Ron, and Tom.

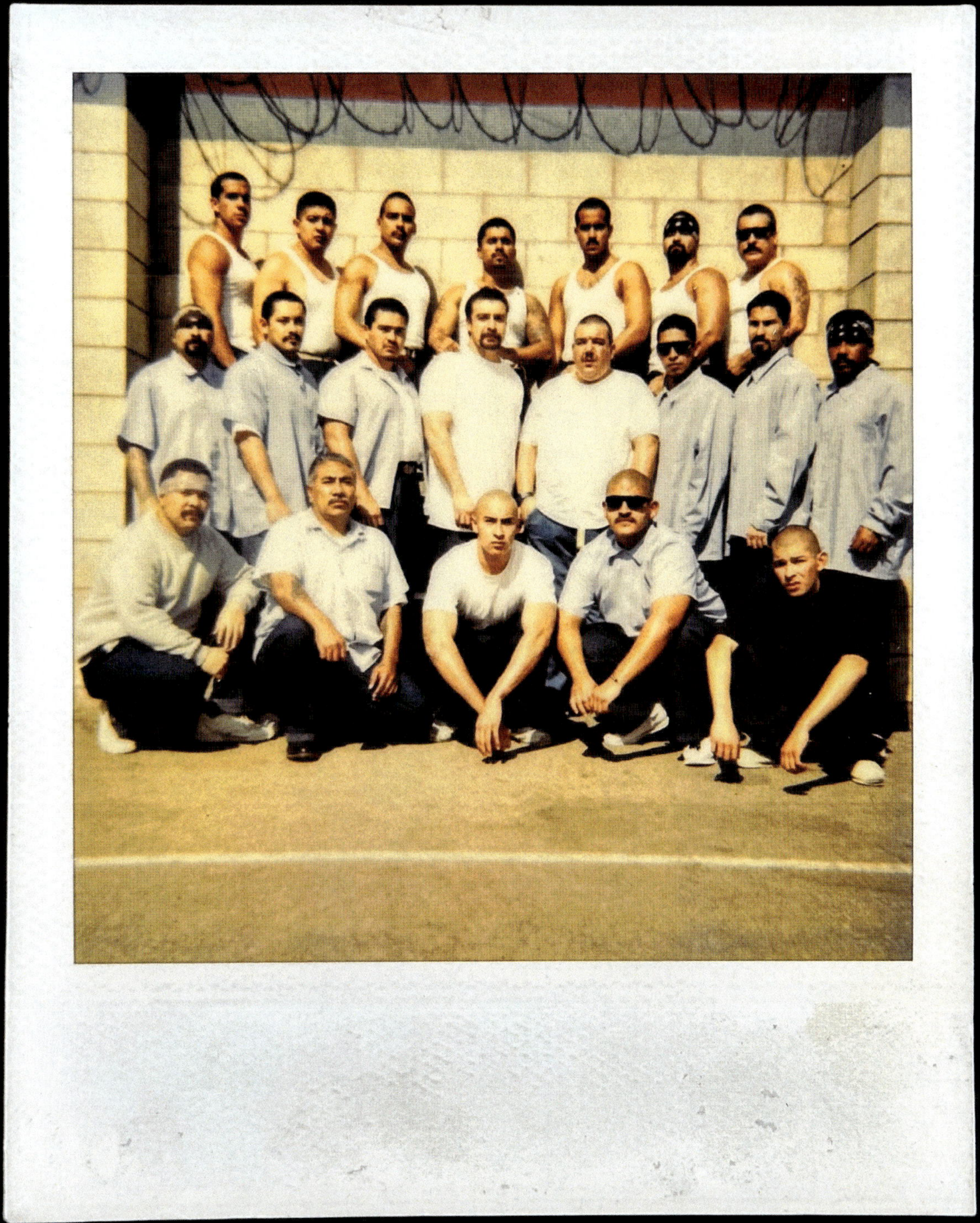

This photo, taken in the mid-1990s, depicts a group of Southerners in classic prison poses. A Southerner is a Hispanic Gang member from Southern California who, in prison, is under the authority of the Mexican Mafia.

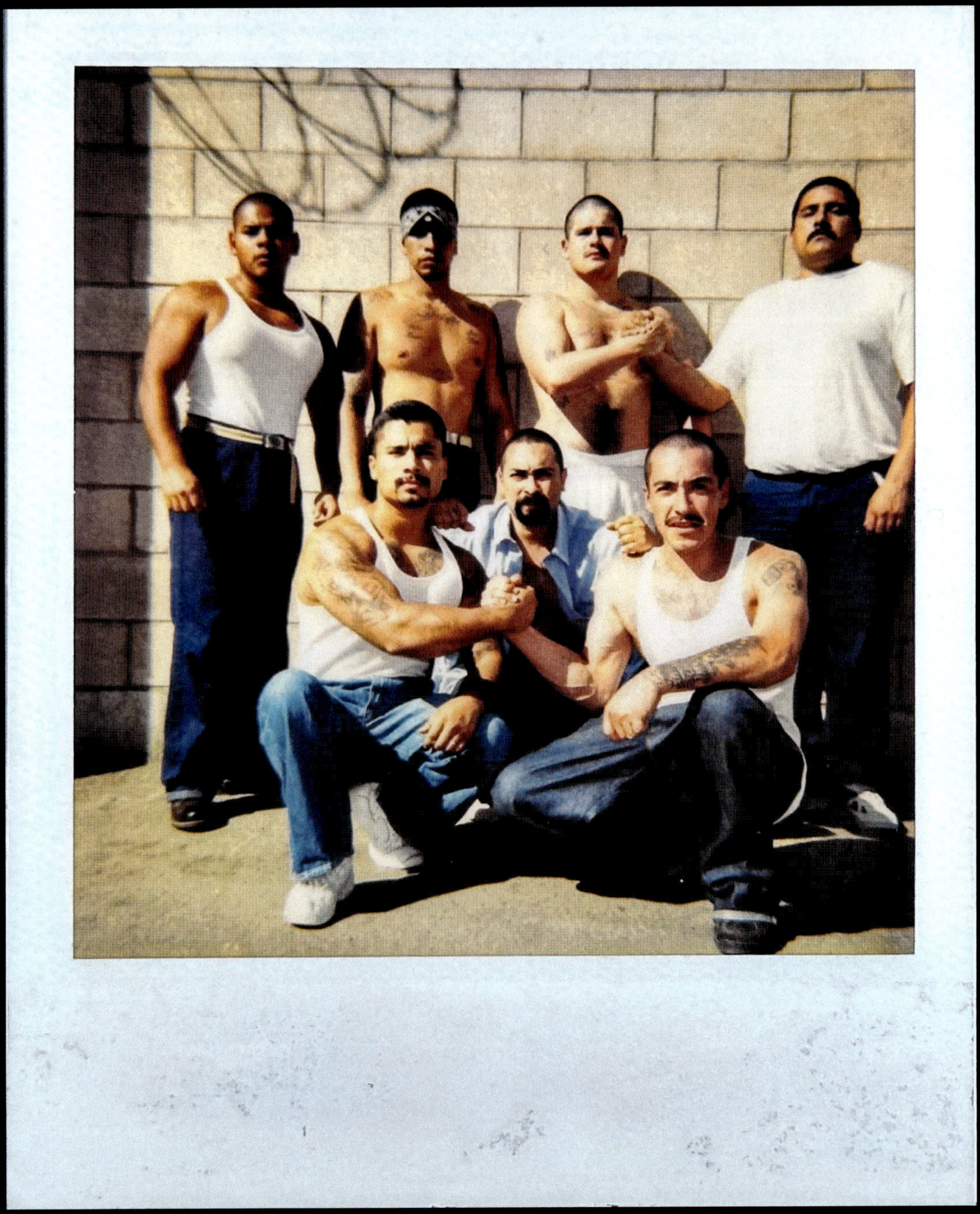

This photo, taken in the mid-1990s, depicts a group of Southerners in classic prison poses. A Southerner is a Hispanic Gang member from Southern California who, in prison, is under the authority of the Mexican Mafia.

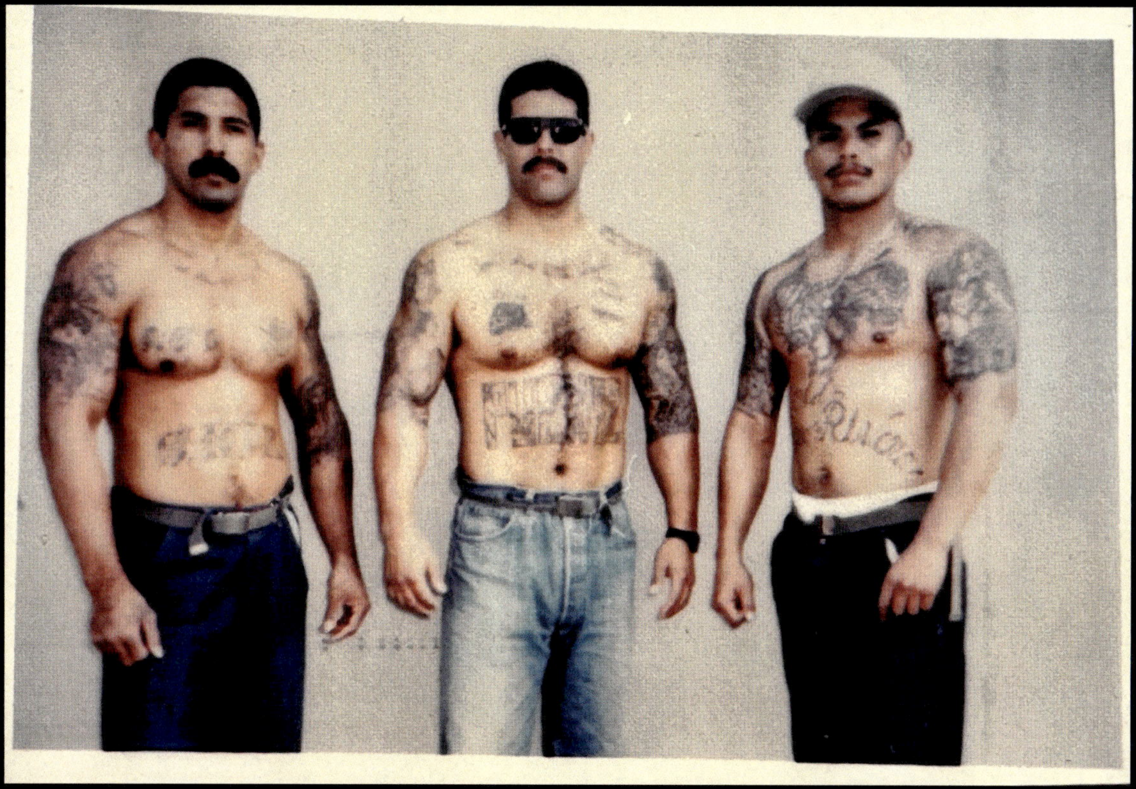

This photo, taken in the mid-1990s, depicts a group of Southerners in classic prison poses. A Southerner is a Hispanic Gang member from Southern California who, in prison, is under the authority of the Mexican Mafia.

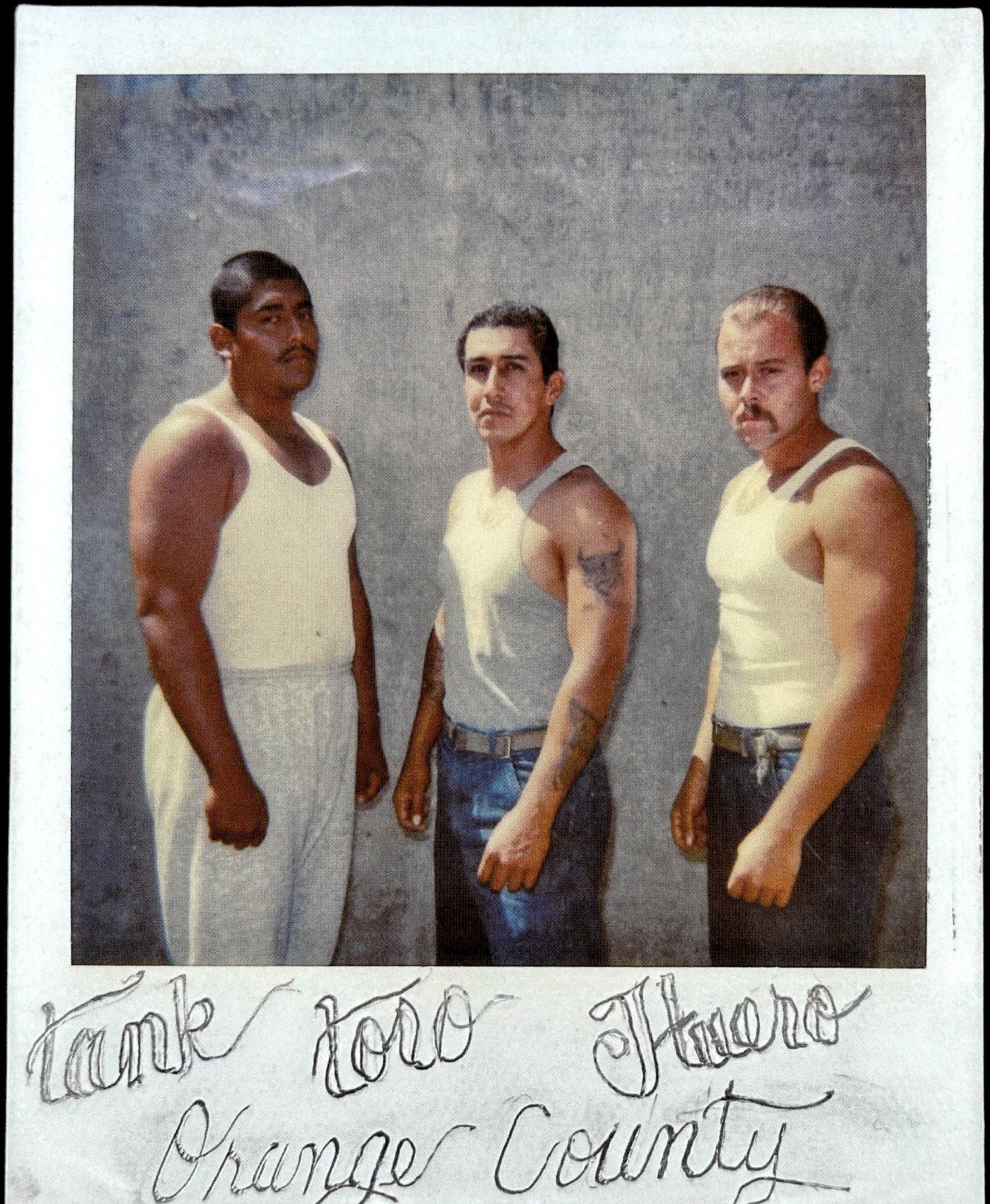

This photo, taken in the mid-1990s, depicts a group of Southerners in classic prison poses. A Southerner is a Hispanic Gang member from Southern California who, in prison, is under the authority of the Mexican Mafia.

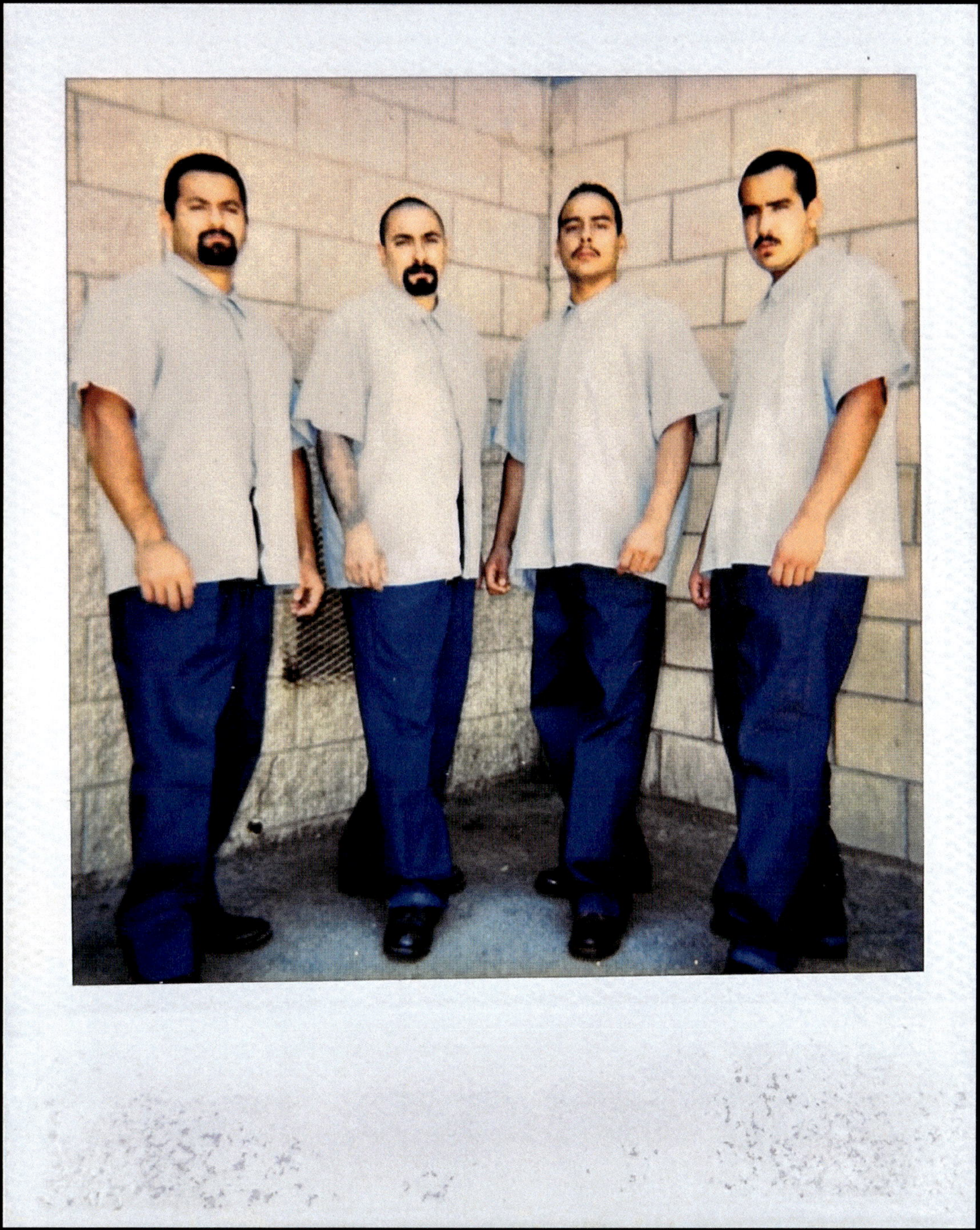

This photo, taken in the mid-1990s, depicts a group of Southerners in classic prison poses. A Southerner is a Hispanic Gang member from Southern California who, in prison, is under the authority of the Mexican Mafia.

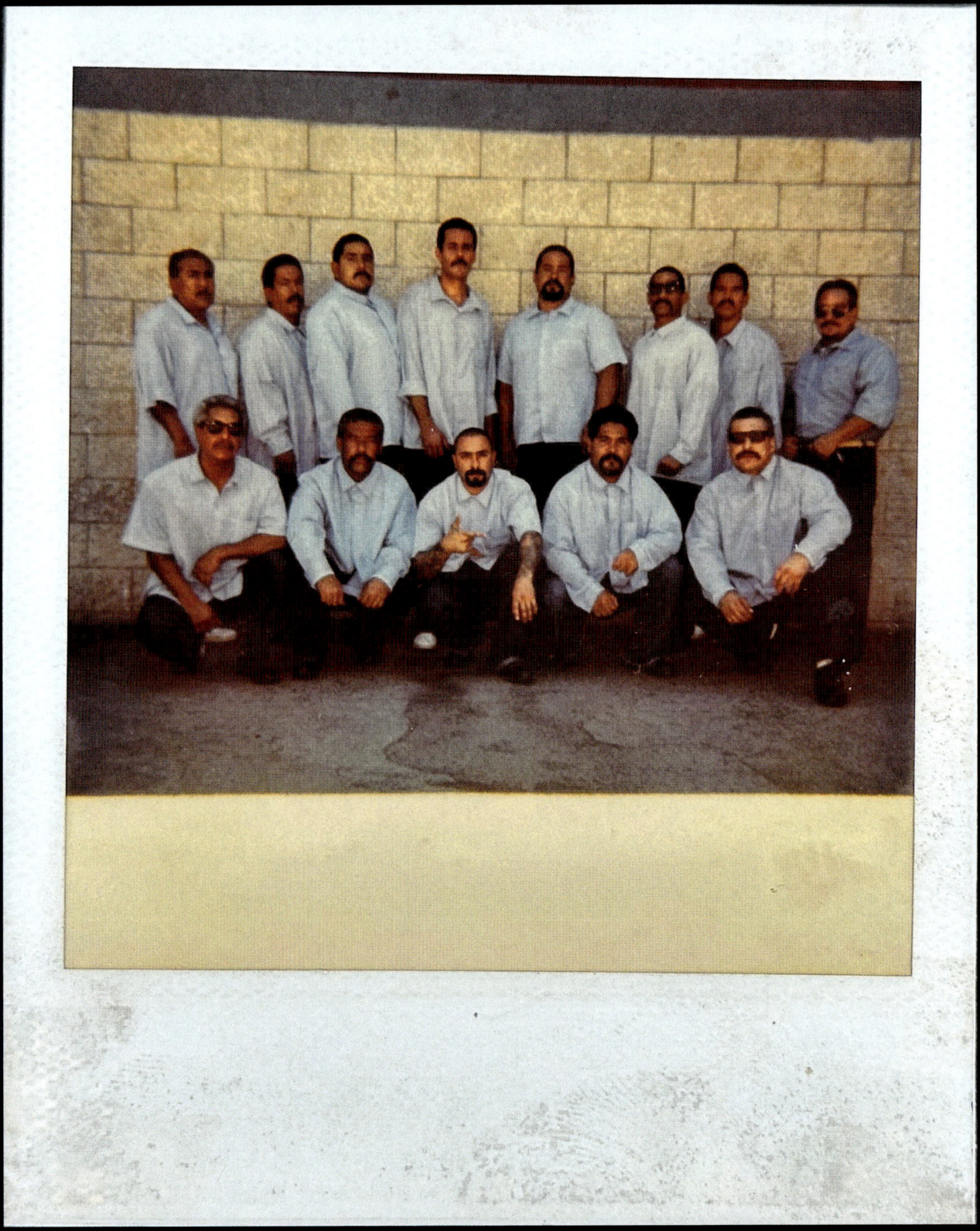

This photo, taken in the mid-1990s, depicts a group of Southerners in classic prison poses. A Southerner is a Hispanic Gang member from Southern California who, in prison, is under the authority of the Mexican Mafia.

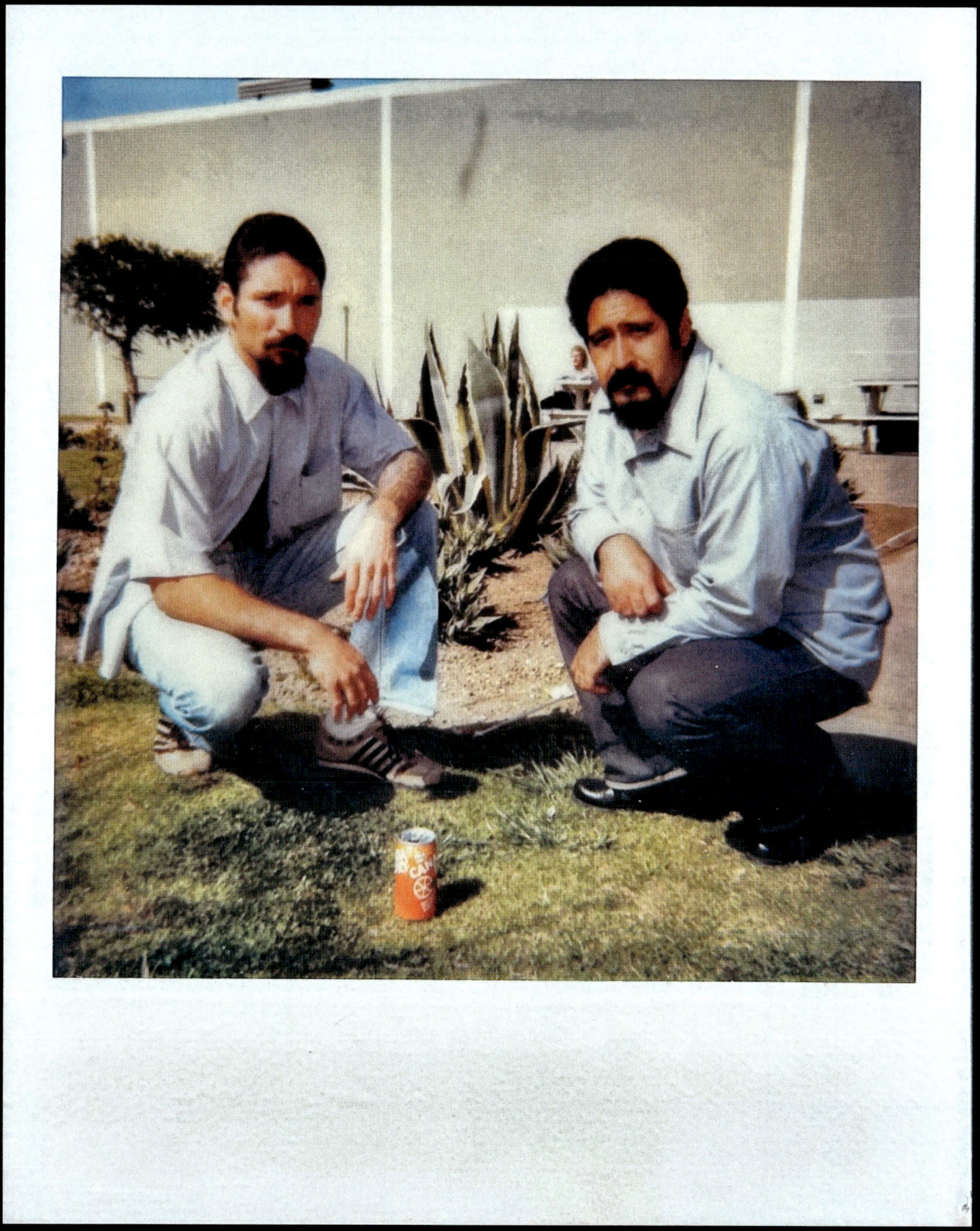

This photo, taken in the mid-1990s, depicts two Hispanic men on a California prison yard.

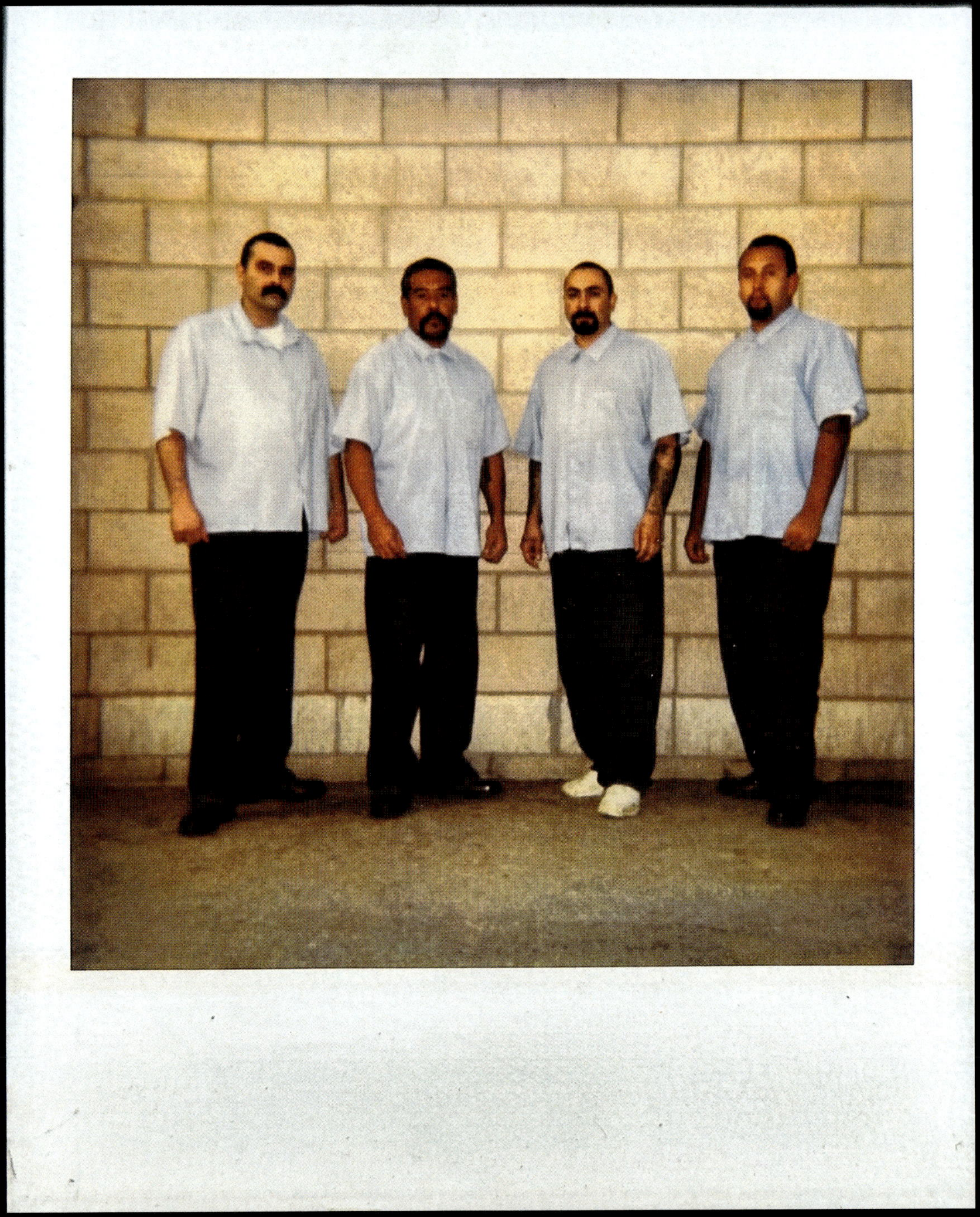

This photo, taken in the mid-1990s, depicts a group of Southerners in classic prison poses. A Southerner is a Hispanic Gang member from Southern California who, in prison, is under the authority of the Mexican Mafia.

About the Author

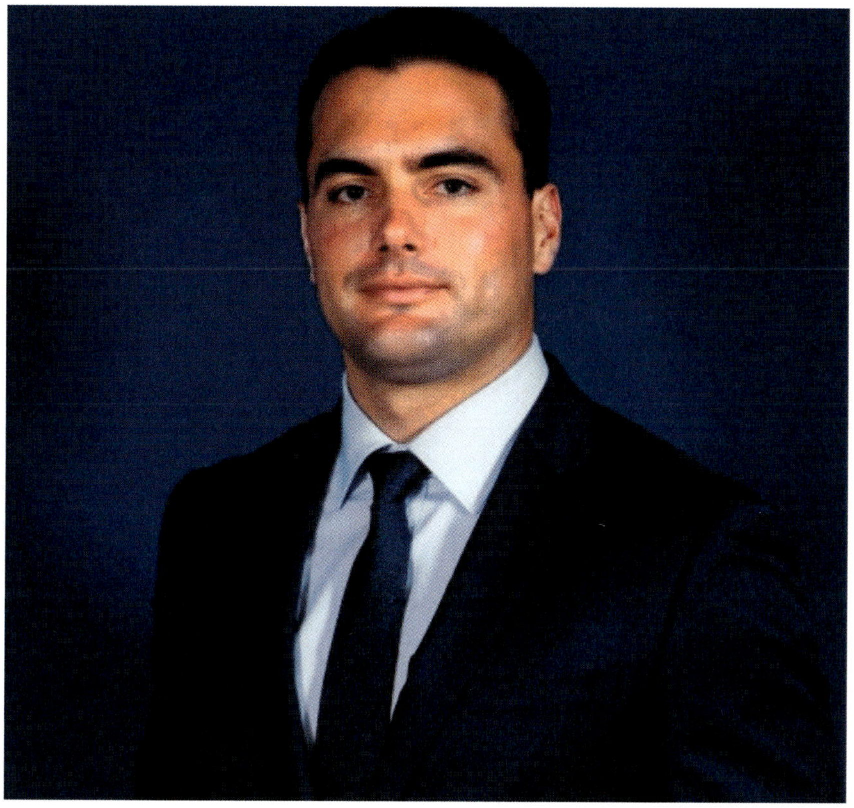

Eric has emerged as a highly accomplished investor and Day Trader, engaging in trading activities with a substantial value of stocks annually. He enjoys the status of a dedicated husband and father, being blessed with four wonderful daughters who hold a special place in his heart. Eric's existence revolves around upholding the virtues of a devout Christian, a devoted husband, and a caring father guided by the grace of God. His journey has been transformative, considering his challenging upbringing, and he now stands as an illustrious testament to the boundless possibilities achievable through faith in God.

Eric joined a criminal street gang as a teenager, and he was eventually arrested and put in a cage at the Long Beach City Jail. He dropped out of Jordan High School in Long Beach, California, in the 10th grade. Eric eventually got on the right path by the grace of God and obtained his GED the same month that he would have graduated. He joined the United States Coast Guard at 18, and after four years of faithful service, he was honorably discharged.

The following is an excerpt from his autobiography: "California Prison Confessions." "It was a typical beautiful summer night in Long Beach, California, and the three young teens fighting in the musty garage starkly contrasted the night's serenity. A teen called Bones was thrown against a wall, and a muscular teenager nicknamed E Double (me) rushed towards him and violently punched him in his lower back. Another youth named Tim Loc held Bones against the wall during this attack. E Double's knuckles landed with a thick-sounding thud as Bones grimaced and moaned in pain from each successive blow.

There's a look of pain and fear in Bone's eyes as E Double mercilessly lands blow after blow to his kidneys. E Double has spent years hitting the heavy bag in his garage, so his punches are devastating for his age. The beating lasted a minute, and the two teens stopped attacking the unfortunate victim. Amazingly, they all shook hands and embraced each other. We were all friends, and this was our modest gang initiation into our small clique called 'Six Feet Under.'"

Our tiny neighborhood gang in North Long Beach, California, had several members of various races: White, Black, and Hispanic. The definition of a criminal street gang according to the California Penal Code is as follows: "As used in this chapter, 'criminal street gang' means any ongoing organization, association, or group of three or more persons, whether formal or informal, having as one of its primary activities the commission of one or more of the criminal acts…having a common name or common identifying sign or symbol, and whose members individually or collectively engage in or have engaged in a pattern of criminal gang activity," California Penal Code 186.22(f).

Some of our associates committed serious crimes such as burglaries, drug sales, stealing cars, carrying guns, vandalism, and assaulting people. Although we were nothing but young punks, we were a criminal street gang according to the California Penal Code.

The FBI did a study entitled "Street-Gang Mentality: A Mosaic of Remorseless Violence and Relentless Loyalty." I want to quote a relevant part concerning young males who do not have a father or other positive male role models in their lives while growing up: "All gang members lacked male role models in their households, and when they lived with their mothers, they were rarely home because of work schedules. Gang members often lived temporarily with various people. All but one gang member reported that one or more immediate family members had a criminal history or abused drugs. Gangs attracted them because of their loyalty, stability, and sense of group identity."

There is an epidemic in this country of boys masquerading as men who don't take their responsibilities as fathers seriously. Many fathers aren't involved in their children's lives; if they are, they are a horrible example of what a real man should be. One of the main factors in young men ending up in the penal system is the lack of a father or, at the very least, a positive male role model when they were growing up. Absentee fathers are causing society to pay a high price for their selfish and callous actions.

Every day, I strive to be the best dad to the four beautiful daughters God has blessed me with. I live by the motto, "Be the man you needed as a child." I will not allow the actions of physically and emotionally abusive people to define who I am or hinder my advancement in life. You can choose to be bitter or better. I strive for excellence because living well is the best response to abusive people.

Eric Sturgess

God bless you and yours.

Romans 10:9-13

For those seeking to connect with Eric or gather additional insights about his upcoming projects, please visit his official website: EricSturgess.com.

Other Books

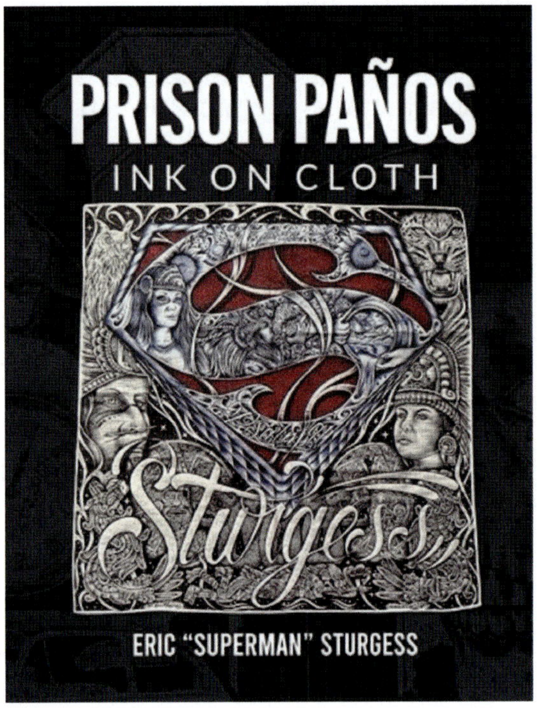

Prison Paños: Ink On Cloth

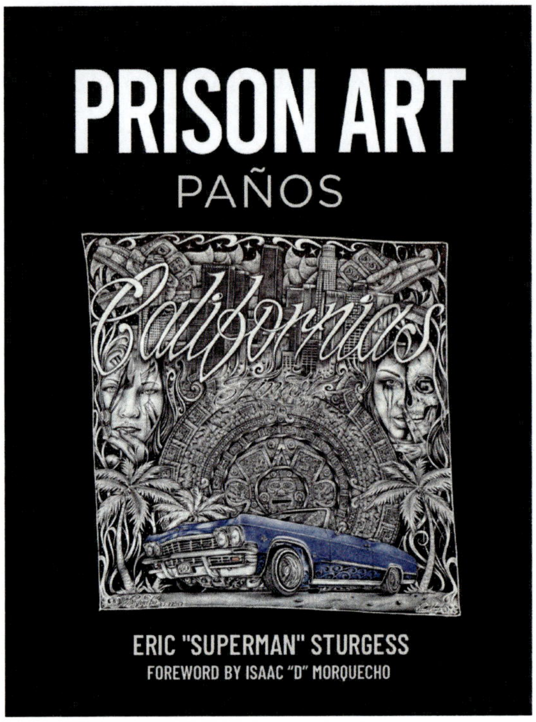

Prison Art Paños

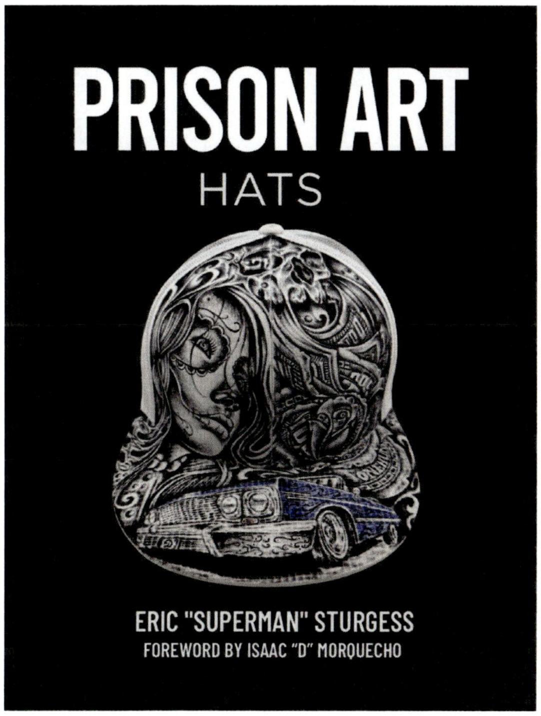

Prison Art Hats

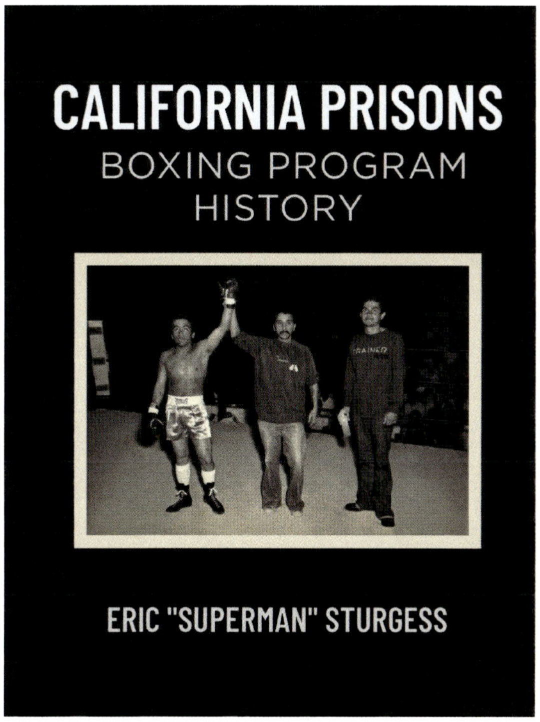

California Prisons: Boxing Program History

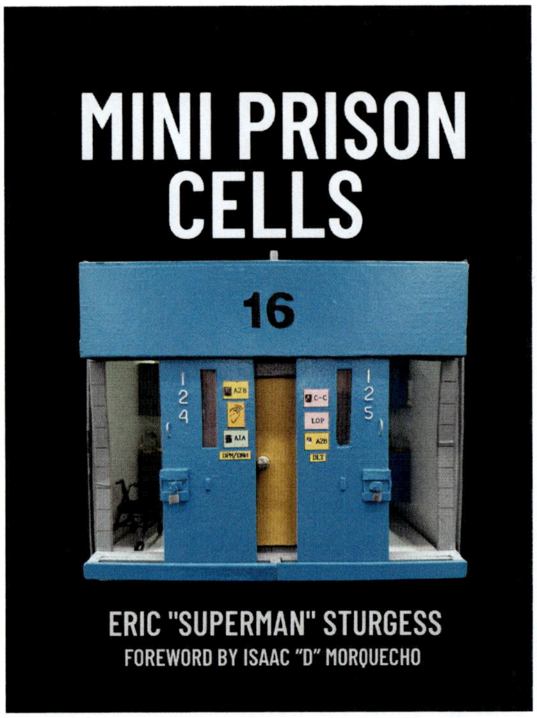

Mini Prison Cells

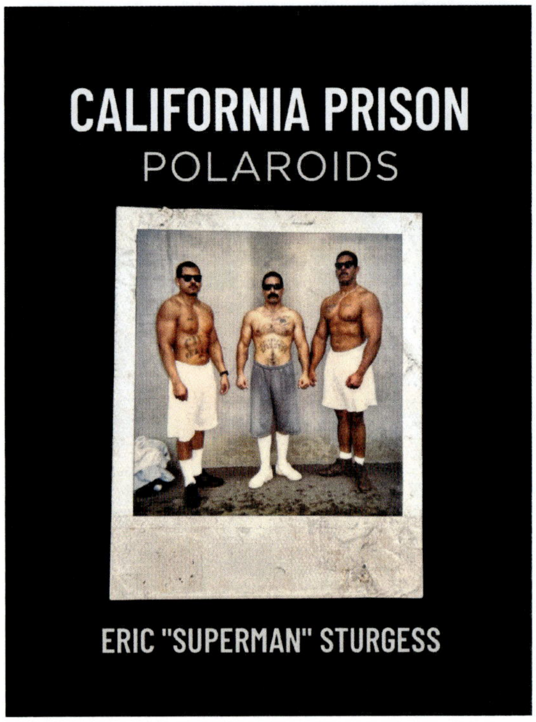

California Prison Polaroids

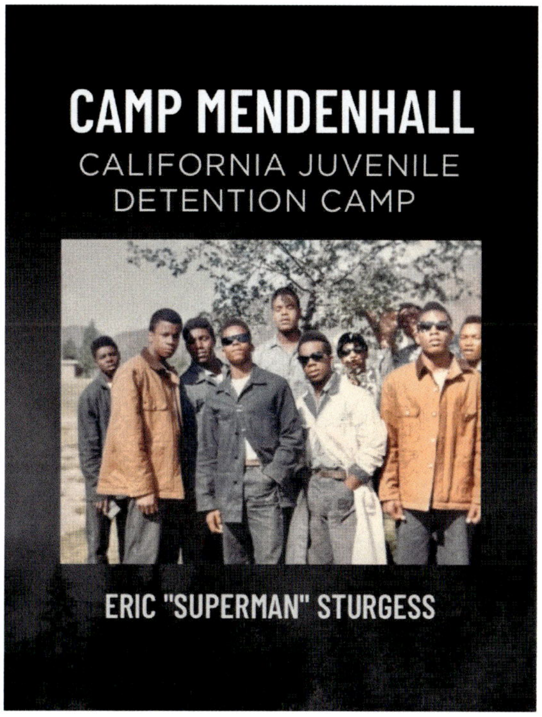

Camp Mendenhall: California Juvenile Detention Camp

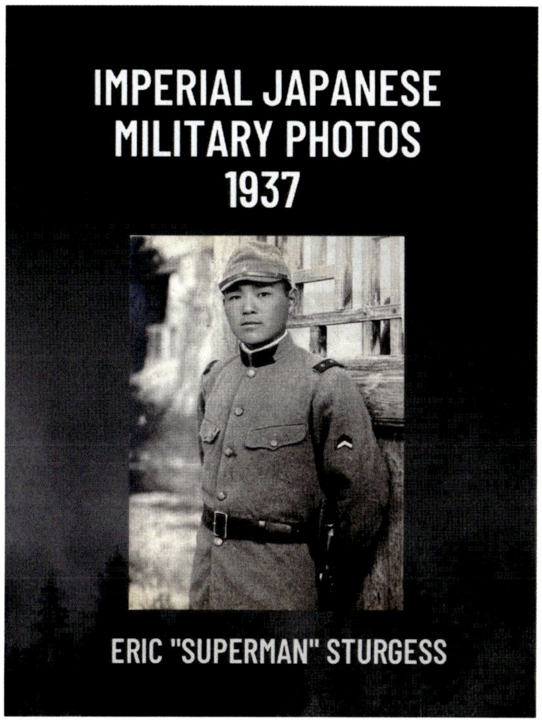

Imperial Japanese Military Photos 1937

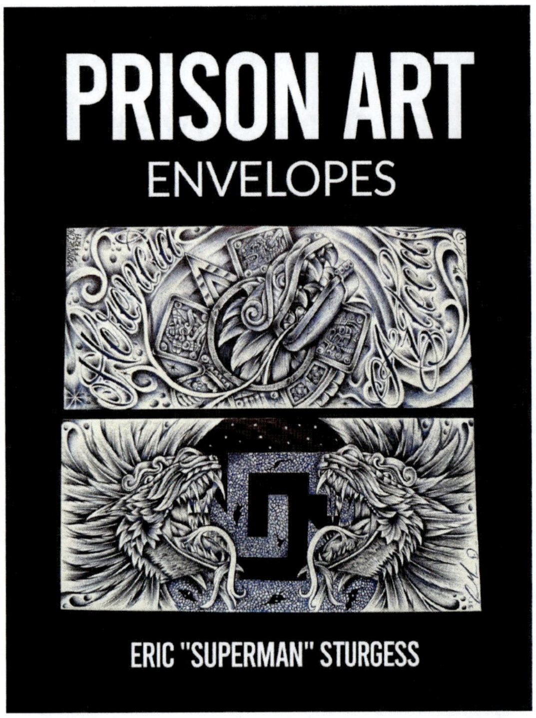

Prison Art Envelopes

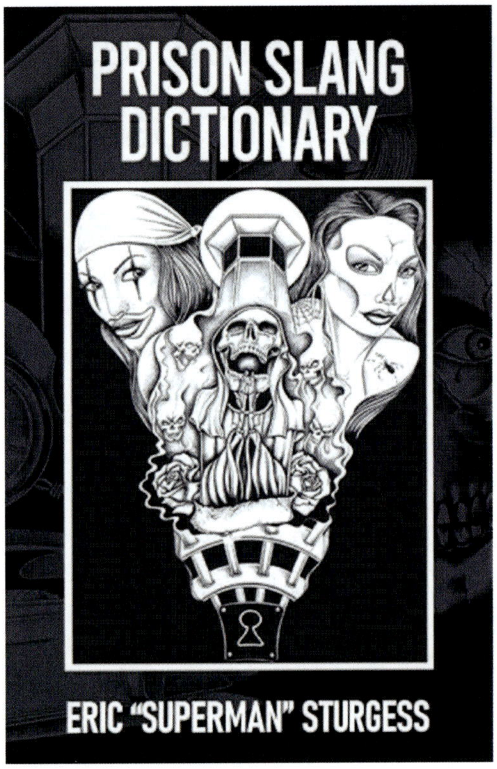

Prison Slang Dictionary